THE WILDFLOWER GARDENER'S GUIDE

Pacific Northwest, Rocky Mountain, and Western Canada Edition

HENRY W. ART

Botanical illustrations by Hyla M. Skudder
Garden illustrations by Elayne Sears
Photographs by the author

A Garden Way Publishing Book
Storey Communications, Inc.
Pownal, Vermont 05261

Cover photograph of Colorado columbie (Aquilegia caerulea) by Henry W. Art
Cover and book design by Andrea Gray
Edited by Deborah Burns
Maps rendered by Northern Cartographic, Inc.
Typesetting by Accura Type & Design, Barre, Vermont
Printed in the United States by Alpine Press

First printing, May 1990

*This book is dedicated to
Meriwether, Richard, and James,
Who came into the Northwest in that order.*

Contents

Acknowledgments

The author and illustrator would like to thank the following people and organizations:

Ken Berg of the California Nongame-Heritage Program, Mark Skinner of the California Native Plant Society, The Virginia Native Plant Society, and California Native Plant Society for aid in framing Wildflower Conservation Guidelines.

Roger Raiche and Jim Affolter of the U. California Botanical Garden, Gayle Weinstein of the Denver Botanic Garden, Rick Brune of the Colorado Native Plant Society, Bob Haller of U. California- Santa Barbara, Barrett Anderson of the Strybing Arboretum and Botanical Garden, and Bart O'Brien of the Yerba Buena Nursery, Woodside, CA, for helpful assistance on botanical issues and scouting sites for wildflower photography.

Dr. R. Stewart Smith, Director of Agricultural Research & Development, LiphaTech for information concerning rhizobium strains.

Walter Kittredge, Michael Canoso, and Emily Wood for assistance in the use of the Harvard University Herbaria (the collections of the Gray Herbarium and Arnold Arboretum).

Chris Skudder for moral support and encouragement, and James Art for his continued hospitality along the way.

Michael Barrow for computer list assistance and Karen Worley, Sawyer Library, Williams College, for computerized literature searches.

David Dethier, Geology Department, Williams College, for his insights into the landscape.

John and Martha Storey and Pam Art for latitude and understanding attitudes.

Deborah Burns for sensitive editing and continued enthusiasm. Andrea Gray and Elayne Sears for design and illustration elements of the project.

Hundreds of people from the botanic gardens, nature centers, arboreta, wildflower seed companies, native plant propagation nurseries, native plant societies, and botanical organizations, who responded to requests for the information contained in the appendices.

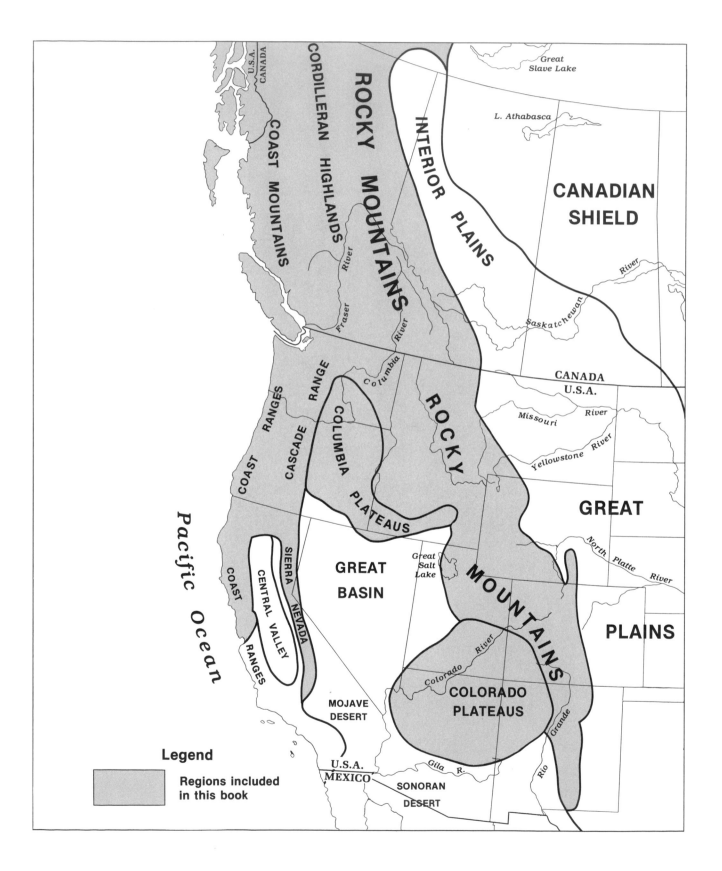

PART I

An Introduction for Wildflower Gardeners

This book is about growing wildflowers in the northwestern corner of North America, a region extending along the Pacific Coast from Central California to Alaska, eastward to the Rocky Mountain chain and southward to New Mexico and the Sierra Nevada. This edition of *The Wildflower Gardener's Guide* focuses on the region from the Pacific Northwest coast to the crests of the western mountains and includes a variety of habitats, ranging from wet coastal forest to montane forest to alpine tundra to open foothill woodlands and grasslands. Of the hundreds of wildflowers that grow in these habitats, 33 of the most easily cultivated and beautiful species have been selected for inclusion in this book. These wildflowers have been chosen to cover the range of flowering season and garden conditions typical of northwestern North America coastal and montane zones.

Wildflowers of Northwestern North America

The Northwest and Mountain West are blessed with a diversity of environmental conditions that make them exciting landscapes in which to live. The dramatic topography of the region, from the Pacific Coast to the Front Range of the Rockies and the crest of the Sierra Nevada, is an environmental stage upon which a vast cast of biological characters puts on a perennial performance of magnificent beauty. I urge you to incorporate the spectacular diversity of native species into your personal landscape — be it containers on a balcony, a modest yard, or a considerable ranch.

Complex climatic patterns and geologic history have contributed to the impressive diversity of native plants that inhabit the region. Less than 35 miles separate 7,954-foot-high Mt. Olympus, where 200 inches of precipitation fall annually, and Sequim, WA, near sea level, where rainfall is less than 20 inches per year. The changes in the physical environment and the resulting changes in types of wildflowers as one travels from the Cascades to the dry Columbia Plateaus or from the high Rockies to the foothills of the Front Ranges are no less impressive.

Some of the climatic extremes of the Northwest coastal and mountain region — torrential winter rains or heavy snows, intense coastal storms, soils that are wet in winter and dry in summer, and periodic fires — can be hard on conventional gardens. Wildflowers provide solutions to many gardening problems since, unlike most domesticated, horticultural plants, they have the ability to make it on their own without human assistance.

WILDFLOWER HABITATS

The native wildflowers of the Northwest are the products of their varied habitats, geologic history, and human activities. Periodic disturbances ranging from fire to ice are natural elements of this mountainous landscape. The face of the Northwest was quite different 15,000 years ago, when the massive ice sheets of the Pleistocene glaciers still covered much of southwestern Canada and mountain glaciers inched along valleys in the Sierra Nevada and Cascades. After the retreat of the ice, the volcanoes of the Cascade Range continued periodically spewing ash and debris over wide portions of the Northwest. The 1914 to 1917 eruptions of Lassen Peak in California and the May 18, 1980 eruption of Mt. St. Helens in Washington are testament to the major natural disruptive forces that continue to work in this geologically "young" landscape. Periodic storms and fires also continually disturb and rejuvenate the landscape. Most importantly, over the past 150 years human activities such as logging, agriculture, grazing, and urban development have altered much of even the steepest terrain in the region. Nevertheless, amid the current patchwork of cities, suburbs, countryside, ranches, farm fields, and clear-cuts are the remnants of the plant communities that have nurtured these wildflowers for millions of years.

North Coastal Forests. Coniferous evergreen forests are found along the Pacific Coast from northern California to Alaska. The trees in these magnificent forests are among the tallest (200 to 300 feet) and oldest (500 to 1,000 years) in North America. The north coastal forests have abundant precipitation, mostly during the winter as storms develop over Hawaii, arc northward through the Gulf of Alaska, and move southward into British Columbia and the Pacific Northwest. The relatively little summer precipitation comes from the infrequent storms moving northward along the Pacific Coast or from fog dripping off branches and needles. Mild temperatures prevail year-round because the North Pacific Current brings water from the warm mid-Pacific to the immediate coast. The abundant moisture and the dominance by conifers produce soils that, while high in organic matter, are generally acidic and poor in nutrients.

In northern California and southern Oregon the coast redwoods (*Sequoia sempervirens*), the tallest trees in the world, tower over an understory of California bay (*Umbellaria californica*), tan oak (*Lithocarpus densiflorus*), and bigleaf maple (*Acer macrophyllum*). Ironically the success of coast redwoods for thousands of years in this damp environment is due to their ability to survive periodic fires; they have thick bark and can resprout after being burned. The species can also produce new roots when its roots are covered by silt deposited during floods.

Farther north along the Pacific Coast, Sitka spruce (*Picea sitchensis*), western hemlock (*Tsuga heterophylla*), and western red cedar (*Thuja plicata*) mingle with Douglas fir (*Pseudotsuga menziesii*) and other conifers, and even some deciduous species such as bigleaf maple. At elevations of 3,000 to 4,500 feet in the north Coastal Ranges where a winter snowpack develops, Sitka spruce and other low-elevation species give way to dominance by Pacific silver fir (*Abies amabilis*), noble fir (*A. procera*), and western white pine (*Pinus monticola*).

Being located close to the Pacific Coast, the north coastal forest is subjected to periodic disturbances, intense winds being only one of them; fire also plays an important role in this type of forest. Every once in several centuries a cat-astrophic fire may appear to destroy a portion of the north coastal forest. More often, less intense fires burn off some of the soil organic matter, creating the conditions needed for the reestablishment of the forest trees. By far the most prevalent present-day disturbance, however, is the human activity of logging in these economically important forests.

Western Montane and Subalpine Forests. Extensive coniferous evergreen forests are also found above the 7,000-foot elevation in the Sierra Nevada, Cascade, Wasatch, and Rocky Mountain ranges, appearing at lower elevations in the northern Rockies than in the southern Sierra Nevada. These regions tend to be warmer in the summer and cooler in the winter than along the Pacific Coast. The montane and subalpine forests generally receive most of their moisture in the form of winter storms, and may have snow accumulations of between 3 and 9 feet. Summer precipitation is sporadic, depending upon the number of southwesterly storm systems that arrive from the Pacific and the local afternoon thunderstorms. The humidity during the summer tends to be low, and the combination of dry air and low rainfall results in relatively frequent fires.

The lower montane forests have a growing season of 4 to 6 months and are dominated by Ponderosa pine (*Pinus ponderosa*), Douglas fir, and other conifer species. Aspen (*Populus tremuloides*) and lodgepole pine (*Pinus contorta*) often invade sites immediately following the fires that occur in the late summer when the soil moisture is depleted. In the Sierra Nevada, giant sequoias (*Sequoia-dendron giganteum*), the largest organisms on earth, and ponderosa pines are usually found in the zone between 6,000 and 8,000 feet. With increasing elevation the growing season shortens to 2 to 3 months, and red fir (*Abies magnifica*) becomes more prevalent in the Sierra Nevada, as does mountain hemlock (*Tsuga mertensiana*) farther north in the Cascade Range and Rocky Mountains.

The subalpine forests extend from the montane forest up to timberline and are frequently interrupted with wet or dry meadows. Subalpine fir (*Abies lasiocarpa*), Engelmann spruce (*Picea engelmannii*), and white-bark pine (*Pinus albicaulis*) are the most abundant species in this zone. Frequently these timberline species, along with bristlecone pine (*Pinus aristata*), grow in a contorted form known as *elfinwood* or *krummholz* near the tops of mountains. Their shrubby stature is a result of being shattered and desiccated by ice-laden winter winds.

Alpine Tundra. At high elevations (above 1,600 feet in northern British Columbia, 9,500 feet in the Sierra Nevada, and 11,500 feet in the Rockies) the environment is so harsh that trees are unable to survive. Here the vegetation is usually a wet, peaty meadow dominated by sedges, rushes (*Luzula spicata*), and alpine grasses (such as *Poa alpina* and *Festuca ovina*). Or it can be a dry, rocky "fellfield" resembling a natural rock garden with a large number of wildflowers and small woody plants such as dwarf willows (*Salix* species) and heath shrubs (*Vaccinium* species) growing as tufted mats.

Not only are winters very cold and frosts possible in any month above the timberline, but solar radiation is nearly 50 percent more intense than at sea level, wind is omnipresent, and soils tend to become quite dry during the summer. The light-reflecting hairy surfaces and ferny shapes of many alpine wildflower leaves are probably adaptations that prevent them from overheating in the summer. Most of the precipitation is in the form of snow; the rate at which the snowpack melts during the spring determines both the length of the growing season and the amount of moisture available for plant growth.

The short growing season (sometimes just a month or two) and stressful environment place a premium on rapid plant growth as the snowpack melts in the late spring. Typically there is then a burst of activity in the alpine tundra, with many species finishing ¾ of their total growth and reaching their flowering peak within 3 weeks of snow melt. Many alpine species rely on starch and sugar produced the previous year and stored over winter in their underground rootstocks to support their rapid growth. Others, like mountain bluebells (*Mertensia ciliata*), which grows in both alpine tundra and subalpine forest clearings, have hollow stems that allow carbon dioxide produced by the respiration of the roots to flow to the top of the plant where it is used in photosynthesis.

Foothills. There is also a "timberline" of sorts at low elevations in the West, where the precipitation is insufficient for forest trees to survive. The transition from montane forest to open foothill woodlands and then to sagebrush generally appears in the rain shadows where the rims of the Great Basin, Colorado, and Columbia plateaus meet the eastern slopes of the Sierra-Cascades and the western slopes of the Rockies, or where the Rockies meet the Great Plains on the east.

As one descends through the foothills the ponderosa pine woodlands become more and more scattered and various species of junipers (*Juniperus occidentalis* in California, *J. osteosperma* in the Great Basin, and *J. monosperma* in the Colorado Plateaus) and piñon pines (*Pinus edulis* and *P. monophylla*) increase in abundance. Interspersed are bunchgrasses such as western wheatgrass (*Agropyron smithii*) and Idaho fescue (*Festuca idahoensis*) as well as cold-desert shrubs.

Cold Deserts. Areas of the Great Basin and western plateaus above 4,000 feet in elevation that receive less than 10 inches of annual precipitation (mostly snow) are known as "cold deserts" because their winter temperatures are generally below freezing. The wildflowers of these areas are discussed in *The Wildflower Gardener's Guide: California, Desert Southwest, and Northern Mexico Edition.*

Grasslands. Areas that receive 10 to 20 inches of precipitation annually, such as the Palouse region and Columbia Basin of Washington and Oregon or the vast floor of California's Central Valley, historically supported natural grasslands that turned from lush green in the spring to golden yellow in the summer. Now these native grasslands support much of the Pacific States' agriculture. The native perennial bunchgrasses such as Indian rice grass (*Oryzopsis hymenoides*), tufted hairgrass (*Deschampsia caespitosa*), bluebunch wheat grass (*Agropyron spicatum*), and Idaho fescue have been replaced by barley, wheat, non-native pasture or hay grasses, and irrigated agriculture. Patches of natural grassland known as "coastal prairie" are also found on south- and west-facing slopes and bluffs of mountains near the Pacific Ocean, and "desert grasslands" are found on the wetter, upslope margins of deserts in the Northwest. The wildflowers of grasslands are discussed in *The Wildflower Gardener's Guide: California, Desert Southwest, and Northern Mexico Edition.*

Chaparral. Rocky, craggy, well-drained slopes near the Pacific Ocean, and occasional inland montane locations, are sometimes covered with thick, often deep-rooted, fire-adapted shrubs known collectively as chaparral. Like grasslands, the chaparral is found in areas with a Mediterranean-type climate of cool, wet winters and warm, dry summers. The montane chaparral is usually dominated by various species of evergreen shrubs such as manzanita (*Arctostaphylos* spp.) and California lilac (*Ceanothus* spp.), as well as many beautiful wildflowers that are described in *The Wildflower Gardener's Guide: California, Desert Southwest, and Northern Mexico Edition.* Fire plays a dominant role in maintaining this type of vegetation, and a given patch of chaparral is likely to burn every 20 years or so.

THE JOYS OF WILDFLOWERS

The beauty of northwestern wildflowers has captivated botanists and gardeners from around the world for several centuries, and Native Americans for thousands of years. While the early European plant explorers cruising the Pacific Coast became enthralled with the new wildflowers they found and eagerly introduced to Europe in the 18th century, it was during the Lewis & Clark Expedition of 1804 to 1806 that the first systematic plant collection of the region was made. Under orders from President Thomas Jefferson, Captains Meriwether Lewis and William Clark were to explore the newly acquired Louisiana Purchase, observing "...the face of the country, its growth and vegetable productions; especially those not of the U.S."

Although he was not a botanist, the list of plants Meriwether Lewis discovered and collected during the expedition is truly impressive: in total, 178 plants not previously described were cataloged. There would have been more, but most of the plants collected and cached east of the Rockies on the westward journey were washed away by flood waters during the winter of 1805-6. Dried plant specimens from the expedition were taken back to the East Coast where botanists named the newly discovered species, some of them in honor of Captains Lewis and Clark. Horticulturlists like Bernard McMahon of Philadelphia grew plants from seeds collected by the expedition and introduced many of these new plants into the garden trade.

Wildflowers Discovered by Lewis & Clark

Rocky Mountain beeplant (*Cleome serrulata*) August 25, 1804, Vermillion River, SD & August 29, 1806, White River, SD

Yellow fawn lily (*Erythronium grandifolium*) May 8, 1806, Nez Perce Co., ID

Blanketflower (*Gaillardia aristata*) "Rocky Mountain dry hills," July 6, 1806, Lewis and Clark Co., MT

Scarlet gilia (*Ipomopsis aggregata*) "On Hungry Creek," June 26, 1806, Idaho Co., ID

Bitterroot (*Lewisia rediviva*) July 1, 1806, Missoula Co., MT

Blue flax (*Linum lewisii*) Valleys of the Rocky Mountains, July 9, 1806, Cascade Co., MT

Tufted evening primrose (*Oenothera caespitosa*) "Near the fall of the Missouri," July 17, 1806, Teton Co., MT

Redwood sorrel (*Oxalis oregana*) March 15, 1806, Ft. Clatsop, OR

Latin and common names of northwestern native plants also reveal the enchantment they held for European botanists like Archibald Menzies, Thomas Nuttall, and David Douglas. Douglas, in whose honor Douglas fir, Douglas's wallflower, and Douglas's iris were named, visited California and the Pacific Northwest several times in the 1820s and 1830s on missions for the Horticultural Society of London. Oregon grape (*Mahonia repens*), California poppy, sky lupine, Chinese houses, purple heliotrope, farewell-to-spring, blazing star, baby blue-eyes, and linanthus were among his discoveries and soon graced British gardens. The blue Washington lupine (*Lupinus polyphyllus*) was introduced into British gardens by David Douglas in 1826. Just over a century later they were hybridized with other species by George Russell, a railroad crossing guard in Yorkshire, England, to produce the world-famous, multicolored Russell hybrid lupines.

Modern-day gardeners can share the botanists' fascination by introducing wildflowers into their own gardens — and even the most common of native species can bring great pleasure as one learns their secrets.

Scarlet gilia. Scarlet gilia (*Ipomopsis aggregata*) is a striking wildflower that graces the dry foothills, montane clearings, and alpine ridges in the Rockies, Sierra Nevada, and Cascades. It grows sometimes as a biennial but more frequently as a monocarpic perennial, living for three to six years and then flowering in a burst of glory, producing seeds, and dying. If fewer than one-third of the flowers are pollinated, however, or if flowering starts late in the summer, scarlet gilia produces a tufted basal rosette that flowers again the next year.

The color and shape of its flowers vary greatly across its range, from bright scarlet to pink to nearly white, and from those with short, broad corolla tubes and projecting stamens to flowers with long, slender corolla tubes completely surrounding the stamens. Some flowers are fragrant, while others are odorless. The most common subspecies *collina*, found predominantly in forest openings, has bright red to pink flowers, while the subspecies *candida*, found mostly in grasslands, has light yellow to white flowers. This species is highly variable, however, and freely hybridizes among its own subspecies and even with other species of *Ipomopsis* with overlapping ranges.

Even though scarlet gilia is pollinated mainly by hummingbirds, its flowers are also visited by white-lined sphinx moths (*Hyles lineata*), beeflies, and short- and long-tongued bees. Hawkmoths visit the red flowers during late afternoon and early evening, and then visit the light-colored flowers at night. Short-tongued bees and beeflies are unable to pollinate the flowers, but rob the nectar by chewing holes in the corolla.

Scarlet gilia produce more nectar during the day when hummingbirds and bees visit the flowers than at night when hawkmoths are active. Even during the day the nectar is rather dilute, so hummingbirds have to visit many flowers to obtain sufficient energy to support their high metabolic rate, a situation that encourages cross-pollination.

The color of scarlet gilia flowers can change during the growing season. In high-elevation sites in Arizona new flowers produced during late July and early August become progressively lighter in color, shifting from darker red to dark pink then light pink and white. These color changes coincide with the migration of hummingbirds away from the area and a shift to hawkmoths as the main pollinator.

Other Species. A wildflower garden may have other delights awaiting discovery. The pealike flowers of Washington lupine (*Lupinus polyphyllus*) have evolved along with the bumblebees that pollinate them (see page 90). The broad upper petal known as the "banner" attracts the attention of the insects, while the two lateral "wing" petals provide landing platforms for them to alight upon. Two lower petals are folded together to form a "keel" that encases the sexual parts. When a bee lands on the wings, it pushes its head against the banner, pries the wings apart with its hind legs, and manipulates the keel with its forelegs. The movement of the keel releases the pistil, which acts like a pump, scooping pollen from the anthers and depositing it onto the bee's abdomen.

Tufted evening primrose (*Oenothera caespitosa*) has large white flowers that open at sunset and reflect the evening moonlight to attract pollinating moths. The following day the flowers fade to pink as they wither in the noonday sun.

During the brief but fascinating late-spring flowering period of the alpine wildflower mountain dryas (*Dryas octopetala*), its white, cup-shaped flowers act like solar collectors, constantly focusing the sun's rays on the pistils, warming them up by as much as 6 degrees F. These sun-warmed flowers attract insect pollinators to bask upon them, ultimately increasing the number and size of fruits. Mountain dryas is self-sterile, so insect pollination is required to produce the seeds. Even though the mountain dryas leaves contain insect-repelling compounds known as glycosides, the larvae of the Alberta fritillary butterfly (*Clossiana alberta*) eat the leaves as their exclusive source of food.

Two different flower forms of sky pilot (*Polemonium viscosum*) are found near the tops of western mountains. The most common one in the alpine tundra near the tops of mountains has large, darker blue flowers with flared corollas and produces a sweet nectar with a floral scent. The other form, found mostly lower on mountains near timberline, has smaller, lighter blue flowers with narrow corollas surrounded by a hairy calyx that emits terpene and flavone compounds with a skunky odor. This odor inspired its common name skunk polemonium. Some sky pilot plants, however, are both skunky and sweet. Different insect pollinators are attracted to the two different scent types. White-lined sphinx moths (*Hyles lineata*) and, especially, queen bumblebees, which emerge each year just as the sky pilot starts to bloom, are attracted to the larger, sweet-smelling flowers and various flics are attracted to the smaller, skunky-scented flowers. Frequently both types of sky pilot can be found growing together, their proportions depending on the types of insect pollinators present.

Fireweed (*Epilobium angustifolium*) is a widely distributed wildflower that frequently is the first to appear after fires, logging, and other disturbances in conifer forests. The magenta flowers of fireweed are pollinated by many species of solitary and colonial bees and bumblebees, especially those in the genera *Bombus* and *Pyrobombus*. Bees forage in an upward spiral direction which leads to cross-pollination. They pollinate flowers in the female phase first and then work their way up to the flowers in the male phase, where they pick up a new load of pollen. Although various butterflies feed on nectar produced in the nectary at the top of the ovary (between the filaments and the style), they are not very effective pollinators.

Blanketflower (*Gaillardia aristata*) often covers the northern Great Plains and openings in foothill woodlands with its red and yellow flowers. The color-banding of its flower heads provides sanctuary for the moth *Schinia masoni*, which has a yellow body and crimson wings. It hides from bird predators during the day with its head pointing toward the tips of the ray flowers and its wings overlapping the red bases of the florets.

This book presents but a few of the hundreds of wildflowers that are worthy of introduction into gardens in northwestern North America. Although some of us greatly enjoy studying those intricacies of wildflower life cycles that can be discovered only through close observation, others may be perfectly content simply appreciating the subtle colors and graceful forms of these elements of our natural heritage.

Getting a Start

This book presents 33 wildflowers native to northwestern North American woodlands and meadows. You may already be familiar with some of these species, such as Washington lupine, harebell, or farewell-to-spring, but others such as Platte River penstemon may be new to you. The selected species are well adapted to the range of conditions likely to exist in gardens of the region and can be propagated without much difficulty. Although any wildflower becomes scarce near the edges of its natural range, none of the species included in this book is designated "rare" or "endangered."* They are generally available from reputable wildflower suppliers who sell nursery-propagated stock, or from seed companies.

It is delightful to watch the parade of wildflowers through the growing season, and the species chosen for this edition will provide a succession of flowering from late winter through autumn. These wildflowers can be grown in a wide variety of conditions, from conventional gardens to woodlands, from meadows to deep shade; some can even be grown in containers on your porch or patio. Hopefully, the wildflowers in this book will be only a starting point for your gardening with native plants.

Many other species are presented in other regional editions of *The Wildflower Gardener's Guide*, *A Garden of Wildflowers* and in other books on native-plant gardening suitable for northwestern North American gardens.

Some wildflowers that are not included in this book are difficult to bring into the garden because of their demanding soil or cultural requirements. Snowplant lacks chlorophyll, for example, and therefore must parasitize the roots of other plants in order to survive. The Indian paintbrushes, which do have green leaves, are nevertheless parasitic on the roots of other plants, and nearly impossible to cultivate in a garden. The mariposa lilies have not been included, because they are generally difficult to grow and because a considerable number of *Calochortus* species are relatively rare. They are best left growing where they

---

* Even though the torreyana variety of sulfur-flowered eriogonum (*Eriogonum umbellatum*) is rare in its small range in California, the species as a whole is very common in the Pacific Northwest and Rocky Mountain region.

WILDFLOWER CONSERVATION GUIDELINES*

1. Let your acts reflect your respect for wild native plants as integral parts of biological communities and natural landscapes. Remember that if you pick a wild-flower, your action affects the natural world. The cumulative effects of the actions of many people can be particularly harmful.

2. Do not collect native plants or plant parts from the wild except as part of rescue operations sponsored by responsible organizations. Even then, any parts, including seeds, of wildflowers on state or federal threatened, rare, or endangered lists cannot be collected without a permit.

3. Encourage the use of regional native plants in home and public landscapes. Before obtaining wild-flower plants or seeds for your home landscape, however, learn enough about their cultural requirements to be sure you can provide a suitable habitat.

4. If you collect seeds from the wild, collect a few seeds or fruits from each of many plants and *only from common species that are locally abundant.* Purchase wildflower seeds only from companies that collect responsibly.

5. Purchase live wildflower plants only from suppliers or organizations that *propagate* their own plants or that purchase their material from those who propagate them. Ask sellers about the origin of the plants you are considering buying. Beware of plants labeled "nursery grown"—they may have been collected from the wild and kept in a nursery for only a short period of time. If there is any doubt about a plant's origin, do not purchase it.

6. Be cautious and knowledgeable in the use of exotic wildflowers. While many non-native species can be attractively used in gardens and landscapes, some are overly aggressive and these weeds may displace native species. Become aware of your state's noxious weed laws by contacting your state Department of Agriculture or Agricultural Extension Service.

7. When photographing wildflowers, or inspecting them closely, be careful not to trample plants nearby. Respect state and local trespassing laws by obtaining permission to be on private land.

8. If you pick wildflowers, dried seed stalks, or greens for home decoration, use only common species that are abundant at the site. Leave enough flowers or seeds to allow the plant population to reseed itself. Avoid picking herbaceous perennials such as wild orchids, mariposa lilies, trilliums, or gentians which, like daffodils, need to retain their vegetative parts to store energy for next year's development. Avoid cutting slow-growing plants such as cacti.

9. Become familiar with your state's wildflower protection laws. If your state does not have laws protecting wildflowers, or if the existing laws are weak, support the passage and enforcement of strong and effective legislation for the preservation of native plants. Report unlawful collection of plants to proper authorities and, when necessary, remind others that collecting plants or disturbing a natural area is illegal in parks and other public places.

10. If you learn that an area with wildflowers is scheduled for development, notify a native plant society in your region. Discuss with the developer the possibilities of compatible development alternatives or, if alternatives cannot be negotiated, of conducting a wildflower rescue operation.

11. It is important to protect information about the locations of rare species. If you discover a new site of a plant species that you know is rare, report it to responsible conservation officials, such as your state's Natural Heritage Program, a native plant society, a Nature Conservancy chapter, or the U.S. Fish and Wildlife Service, as soon as possible and before discussing it with others.

* Adapted from the Virginia Native Plant Society's "Wildflower Conservation Guidelines," with modifications suggested by the California Native Plant Society.

are in the wild and should be moved into your garden only if they are in imminent danger of destruction by development.

WILDFLOWER CONSERVATION

One safeguard of our native wild plants is the Federal Endangered Species Act of 1973, administered by the U.S. Fish and Wildlife Service. This act gives protection to those native species that are recognized as endangered in the United States. This law applies only to federal lands, however, and to the interstate traffic of rare plants. The protection of endangered wildflowers on other public and private lands is left up to the states, as is the protection of species that might become locally rare or endangered through collection by native-plant suppliers and wildflower fanciers. State laws protecting wildflowers are far from uniform, and even where there is protective legislation, the enforcement of these laws is sometimes weak.

Wildflower gardeners should become aware of their state's laws concerning the protection of native plants. If your state lacks such protective legislation, or if the enforcement of the laws is weak, become an advocate for passage of strong and effective measures. The World Wildlife Fund and the Environmental Defense Fund, whose addresses can be found in Appendix C, can provide information concerning model native-plant protection legislation.

The wildflower gardener is faced with moral and ethical considerations that do not confront the gardener of cultivars. Essential to the enjoyment and appreciation of wild, native plants is a respect for living organisms in their native habitats. The wildflower gardener's code of conduct should protect naturally occurring populations of native plants, not only so that others can enjoy them, but also to preserve the ecological roles these plants play. Individual actions do make a difference, both positively and negatively. Wildflower gardeners have the chance to counteract the tragedy of habitat destruction and reduction in native-plant populations occurring around the world.

PLANTING STOCK

One of the first questions one might ask is where to obtain seeds or plants to start a garden of wildflowers. Where *not* to obtain plants is easier to answer. *Plants growing in their native habitats should never be dug up for the garden.* Apart from the laws that protect wildflowers in many states, it is unethical to uproot native plants. Furthermore, many deeply rooted perennials are nearly impossible to transplant even with a backhoe.

The propagation instructions given for the 33 species of wildflowers in this book are intended for gardeners who desire to make divisions of their own plants only, not of those growing in the wild. The only circumstance in which it is acceptable to dig up wildflowers is when they are imminently threatened by highway development or construction, and preservation on the site cannot be arranged. In those cases, prior approval must be obtained from the proper authorities, and if possible, plants should be dug while dormant.

Nursery-grown material usually yields the best wildflower gardening results. Before ordering plants by mail or from a local retail outlet, determine whether the plants have been propagated in a nursery, not merely "grown" there for a while. Do not buy plants that have been collected in the wild, since this practice may deplete natural populations of plants deserving protection. When ordering wildflowers you may wish to purchase seeds or live plants from a producer who is relatively close by, since there is a greater likelihood that the stock is better adapted to your local environmental conditions.

Two species in this book, yellow fawn lily (*Erythronium grandiflorum*) and giant trillium (*Trillium grandiflorum*), are not considered to be "economically viable" species for commercial nurseries to grow. While they are relatively easy to grow from seed, and do self-seed in the wild, it may take more than 5 years for plants from seed to grow to flowering size, and therefore nurseries generally cannot afford the cost of producing them. These beautiful additions to the garden are presented in this book only for those willing to grow them from seed and those with the patience to wait a half-decade for their rich reward. If you find a nursery that sells live fawn lilies or trilliums, be especially careful to determine that they were indeed propagated there rather than collected from the wild.

Seeds. Much can be gained by propagating wildflowers by seed, even apart from seeds' year-round availability, durability in shipping, and relatively low cost. Raising wildflowers from seed gives the gardener a chance to become familiar with the complete life cycle of plants. Some of the species in this book will self-seed once established, and therefore it is useful to know from firsthand experience what the seedlings of the species look like. Often the leaves of seedlings look different from those of mature plants, and without this knowledge they might be accidentally removed as weeds.

You can collect the seeds of most perennials growing in the wild without fear of significantly affecting their populations, if you take only a small proportion of the seeds produced. Since annuals reproduce only by seed, collect seeds from them only in locations where their populations are abundant. Before collecting any seeds get permission from the property owner.

Wildflower seeds are usually available throughout the year from mail-order suppliers. Some perennial wildflowers of northwestern North America have enhanced germination when their seeds are chilled or *stratified* for several months. Check with the supplier to determine whether the seeds you purchase have been pretreated or if they would benefit from additional cold treatment.

Wildflower Seed Mixtures: Caution! You should be very cautious and fully informed before purchasing commercial wildflower seed mixtures, which recently have been gaining popularity. Some suppliers painstakingly formulate mixtures that are representative of native wildflowers of specific regions or habitats. Others, however, formulate mixes for broad geographic regions and may include species that are not particularly adapted to your local conditions. Furthermore, it is often difficult to know just what species are contained in some of the mixtures and in what proportions. Some of the producers of the wildflower mixtures will vary the composition depending upon the temporary availability of seeds, so there is no guarantee that the product will be uniform from year to year. Often the mixes contain an abundance of annuals that provide a splash of color the first year but have difficulty in reseeding themselves. The lack of perennials in these mixes may mean disappointment in subsequent years. As long as you are investing in wildflowers, you might as well pay for only what you want, not just a pretty can or a packet mostly of roadside weeds.

A further difficulty with some of the mixes is the inclusion of weedy, nonnative wildflower species which, while attractive, may become aggressive. An analysis of various wildflower seed mixes by the New England Wild Flower Society in 1985 found them to be comprised of eight to thirty-four different species, of which zero to 100 percent were native. The following are some non-native species that are commonly found in wildflower mixes:

SPECIES	PLACE OF ORIGIN	SPECIES	PLACE OF ORIGIN
Oxeye daisy	Europe	Dame's rocket	France
Corn poppy	Europe	African daisy	South Africa
Sweet alyssum	Europe–W. Asia	Foxglove	Europe
White yarrow	Europe	Candytuft	S.E. Europe– W. Asia
Baby's breath	S. Europe	Four-o'clock	Peru
Purple loosestrife	N. Europe	Queen Anne's lace	Europe
St. John's-wort	Europe–Africa	Chicory	Europe
Bouncing bet	Europe–Asia	Cornflower	Europe

Live Plants. Since it often takes several years for perennial wildflowers to bloom when started from seed, the fastest way to establish them in the garden is to purchase live plants from reputable suppliers. Planning is essential. Perennial wildflowers are best shipped and planted when they are dormant. Many mail-order suppliers ship only during a limited season, so you should contact suppliers to determine the season of availability and whether there are any other constraints in shipping the specific live wildflowers you wish to plant.

SUPPLIERS   The number of reputable commercial producers and distributors of wildflower plants and seeds is steadily increasing, especially in metropolitan areas of the Northwest. Some commercial sources are listed in Appendix A, although their inclusion is in no way an endorsement by the author or publisher. Most suppliers have catalogs or lists giving prices of seeds, live plants, and other items useful in wildflower gardening. Many of these catalogs are extremely useful sources of information about growing native plants. As is noted in Appendix A, some of the suppliers have a small charge for their catalogs and some refund that charge with the first order. It is a good idea to order catalogs several months in advance of your anticipated planting time. Some suppliers have shipping restrictions across international boundaries, and where these are known they are mentioned in Appendix A. Most suppliers prefer payment in the currency of their own country, and some require it.

If you are planning to plant large areas with mature bulbs and rootstocks, some of the suppliers listed in Appendix A sell large quantities of live plants (and seeds) to the public at wholesale prices. Although many suppliers give wholesale discounts to the public, some sell at wholesale rates only to registered retailers, so check with the supplier first.

MORE   This book may be just a beginning for you. Further information is available
INFORMATION   from many sources, some of which are listed in the appendices to this book.

Botanical Gardens. Botanical gardens, nature centers, and arboreta are excellent sources of information about gardening with native plants. A state-by-state listing of such institutions is given in Appendix B. This listing includes the admission fee, if any, the season of operation, and the phone numbers. The resources of these gardens and centers usually extend beyond their collections of living native plants. Many offer workshops, symposia, tours, or lecture series on wildflower gardening. Some publish magazines, newsletters, and brochures that include information on native plants, and they often have shops that sell books on wildflowers as well as wildflower seeds and live plants.

Many botanical gardens offer memberships that entitle members to use library facilities, attend special events at reduced prices, go on field trips to various natural areas, consult with the horticultural staff, use a phone "gardening hotline," and enjoy other benefits. If you become interested in the institution's activities, they may have a program in which you could become a volunteer.

There are numerous other places not listed in Appendix B to observe wildflowers. Many local, regional, state, and national parks have preserved areas of native vegetation. National Forests and National Wildlife Refuges are also ideal places to see native wildflowers, as are lands owned by various chapters of the Audubon Society and the Nature Conservancy.

Botanical Organizations. Native plant societies and some horticultural organizations are excellent sources of information about native plants, as well as a means of becoming involved with wildflowers. The activities and resources of these societies are quite varied, ranging from projects to conserve rare and endangered plants to field trips, lecture series, and seed exchanges. Many of the native plant societies periodically publish newsletters or bulletins and have smaller local chapters that hold regular meetings. Some of the societies are affiliated with specific botanic gardens or arboreta, while others have a more regional or national focus. Appendix C lists botanical organizations that are concerned with wildflowers.

One organization concerned with native plants across the continent is the National Wildflower Research Center, located in Austin, Texas. The N.W.R.C., founded in 1982, is a clearinghouse for wildflower information, an institution conducting research on the propagation and cultivation of native plants, and an advocate for wildflower conservation and preservation. The public is encouraged both to contact the N.W.R.C. for information about native plants and to join them in their cause. The address of the National Wildflower Research Center is given in Appendix C.

On a state level, most states in the northwestern United States have Natural Heritage Programs, cooperative efforts between the Nature Conservancy and state departments of fish and game or natural resources to take inventory of rare plants, animals, and biological communities. The first Natural Heritage Program was started in South Carolina in 1974, to provide that state with biological inventory data augmenting the Federal Endangered Species Act. The offices of Natural Heritage Programs listed in Appendix C can provide you with current information on rare and endangered wildflowers and plant communities in your state.

The National Council of State Garden Clubs, Inc. is also active in wildflower preservation, and advocates using native plants for landscaping roadsides and public spaces. The organization sponsors "Operation Wildflower," a cooperative effort among state garden club federations, state highway agencies, and the Federal Highway Administration to beautify the nation's highways with native species, providing a low-cost, low-maintenance alternative to the exotic grasses and weeds that dominate our roadsides. Since its inception in 1972, Operation Wildflower has extended its horizons beyond the roadside to include projects in public parks, gardens, and wildflower preserves.

References. An annotated bibliography of books and published resources on wildflower gardening is contained in Appendix D.

Theme Gardens

Cultivating native wildflowers of northwestern North America can open new horizons in low-maintenance gardening. A sense of satisfaction accompanies the reestablishment of plants that were once more widespread in the region. Whether you use native plants to complement existing gardens or establish new plantings of species with different environmental requirements, you don't have to start out on a grand scale. Some of the most successful wildflower gardens are small flower beds at the corner of a house or on small patches of land otherwise unused. Even those areas that you can't mow anyway between the roots of the trees in the front yard can be enhanced by plantings of wildflowers.

Wildflowers let you adapt landscapes for specific purposes, such as "xeriscaping" to reduce water consumption by planting drought-tolerant plants, or planting wildflowers as ground covers in areas too shady for lawns. Wildflowers can also be used in more natural settings. Alpine plants are naturally adapted to grow in rock gardens, even at lower elevations. Foothill woodlands can be enhanced through the addition of wildflowers adapted to that habitat. Similarly, you can beautify montane and coastal areas by planting appropriate species of native wildflowers.

HORTICULTURAL GARDENS

Beds and Borders. The simplest approach is to use wildflowers in existing gardens to complement your ornamental plants. Conventional flower beds might include species such as farewell-to-spring, blanketflower, and Mexican hat, whose long stems and long-lasting flowers make them ideal cut flowers.

Many western native plants are ideal for sunny borders. Tufted evening primrose, sky pilot, and sulfur-flowered eriogonum, with their low growth forms and interesting foliage, make excellent border plants. If your border is shady, try western bleeding hearts or western solomon's seal.

Butterfly and Hummingbird Gardens. If you want to attract butterflies to your garden, plant species such as Colorado columbine, mountain dryas, blanketflower, and Mexican hat, which have contrasting flower colors or sweet nectars to attract adult butterflies. Another approach is to plant wildflowers that the developing caterpillars like to eat. The larvae of small butterflies known as "blues" eat lupines as their main food, and West Coast lady butterflies eat checker bloom and other members of the mallow family. One obvious reason to refrain from using insecticides in wildflower gardens is the harm they cause to butterflies.

Hummingbirds are attracted to red or pink flowers that point outward or hang down. To lure hummingbirds to your garden, try planting scarlet gilia and leopard lily. Bees are attracted to wildflowers such as western monkshood, mountain bluebells, and elephantheads, whose shapes fit their bodies, or to flowers

A. Fireweed
B. Washington lupine
C. Colorado columbine
D. Scarlet gilia
E. Pearly everlasting
F. Sulfur-flowered eriogonum

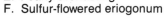

Butterfly garden.

Western Wildflowers for Butterflies

Wildflower	Butterfly
Colorado columbine	Many
Pearly everlasting	American painted lady (*Vanessa virginiensis*)
Rocky Mountain beeplant	Checkered white (*Pontia protodice*) Western white (*P. occidentalis*)
Western bleeding hearts	Clodius parnassian (*Parnassius clodius*)
Mountain dryas	Alberta fritillary (*Clossiana alberta*)
Fireweed	Blueberry sulphur (*Colias pelidne*)
Sulfur-flowered eriogonum	Blue copper (*Chalceria heteronea*) Desert green hairstreak (*Callophrys comstocki*) Immaculate green hairstreak (*C. affinis*) White-lined green hairstreak (*C. sheridanii*) Acmon blue (*Icaricia acmon*) Lupine blue (*I. lupini*)
Blanketflower	Dakota skipper (*Hesperia dacotae*) Skipper butterfly (*Atryomopsis hianna*)
Scarlet gilia	White-lined sphinx moth (*Hyles lineta*) Swallowtail butterfly (*Papilio rutulus*)
Blue flax	Variegated fritillary (*Euptoieta claudia*)
Washington lupine	Sooty hairstreak (*Satyrium fuliginosum*) Silvery blue (*Glaucopsyche lygdamus*) Orange-bordered blue (*Llycaeides melissa*) Common blue (*Icaricia icarioides*) Acmon blue (*Icaricia acmon*)
Checker bloom	West coast lady (*Vanessa annabella*)
Mexican hat	Dakota skipper (*Hesperis dacotae*) Poweshiek skipperling (*Oarisma poweshiek*)

with sweet nectar and contrasting colors. Planted as companions to those that attract butterflies, these wildflowers will provide a long season of winged guests.

Ground Covers. Some of the native species in this book make superb ground covers and are effective in controlling erosion. To stabilize sunny banks and steep areas prone to erosion, plant perennials such as fireweed, Oregon grape, and pearly everlasting with their deep and spreading roots, along with native grasses and shrubs. Bunchberry, western bleeding hearts, redwood sorrel, and western Solomon's seal make attractive ground covers for cool, moist shady areas that aren't subjected to foot traffic.

Rock Gardens. No rock garden is truly complete without representative native species. By their very nature, alpine and some foothill species are adapted to rock garden conditions. When using wildflowers you can create rock gardens for sun or shade, and for moist or dry conditions. Take the environmental preferences of various wildflowers into consideration when planning your rock garden.

Plant pearly everlasting, bitterroot, farewell-to-spring, sulfur-flowered eriogonum, tufted evening primrose, scarlet gilia, and penstemons in dry, sunny places such as the south-facing exposure near the top of the garden. Colorado columbine, on the other hand, prefers partial shade and might be planted on east- or west-facing slopes. Checker bloom should be planted low in cool nooks of the rock garden so it can gain a bit more moisture than other rock-garden plants. Harebell is not too choosy about the site, except that it, like the other rock-garden species, requires well-drained soils. If you are planting a rock garden in the humid Pacific coastal region, pay careful attention to drainage. In sites with damp soils the rock garden should be built around a central core of sandy, gravelly soil to facilitate drainage. If you have a large space for a rock garden you might consider growing more aggressive wildflowers like fireweed.

Container Gardening. Growing wildflowers in containers is an easy way to enjoy native plants if you live in a city, if your gardening space is limited, or if more intensive care is needed because your local conditions are quite different from those usually required by a particular species. One advantage to container gardening is that you can move the plants seasonally, indoors or out, to match the needs of the species. When farewell-to-spring or leopard lily are planted densely in large containers they provide stunning accents for courtyards, balconies, or patios. Wooden or masonry boxes planted with the low-growing western bleeding hearts, Oregon grape, or sulfur-flowered eriogonum are especially attractive along side paths and stairways.

Redwood sorrel is well suited for growing in cool, shady terrariums or even hanging baskets. It has attractive foliage, creeping stems that grow to overflow the sides of baskets, and small, attractive white or lavender flowers.

A wide variety of containers can be used: conventional pots, wooden tubs, window boxes, hanging baskets, drainage tile, and chimney flue liners, to mention a few. Containers made of porous ceramic material, like clay pots, tend to dry out faster, so wildflowers planted in them need to be watered more frequently than those planted in impervious glass, glazed ceramic, or plastic containers.

Wildflowers That Attract Bees

Western monkshood
Oregon grape
Rocky Mountain beeplant
Sulfur-flowered eriogonum
Mule's ears
Blanketflower
Mountain bluebells
Washington lupine
Checker bloom
Elephantheads
Tufted evening primrose
Giant evening primrose
Yellow fawn lily

Ground covers.

A. Western Solomon's seal
B. Western bleeding heart
C. Bunchberry
D. Oregon grape
E. Redwood sorrel

Good drainage is essential for container gardening, since water-logged soils not only prevent the roots from getting needed oxygen, but also encourage diseases. Many plants adapted to dry soil conditions simply cannot tolerate wet soils. First, be sure the container has a drainage hole, and line the bottom of the pot with a layer of pot shards or gravel. The soil you use should be light and porous. Equal measures of top soil, peat moss, and builder's sand, mixed thoroughly, make a good potting mixture for most plants. With the plant in place, the pot should be filled to about 1 inch from the top with this loamy soil mix.

The root growth of plants in containers tends not to be as extensive as that of plants growing in conventional gardens, so additional water is usually required. Water the container garden only after the surface of the soil has become dry to the touch, and then water sufficiently for water to drain out and carry the dissolved salts out the drainage hole. Otherwise, salts may build up in the soil and damage the plants. Regular watering will remove some of the necessary plant nutrients from the soil, so periodically add small amounts of slow-release fertilizers to replace them.

NATURAL GARDENS AND LANDSCAPES

A highly successful way to use native plants is to plant wildflowers in appropriate natural settings. This also allows you to brighten up areas of your property that are difficult to plant, such as beaches, fire-prone areas, and dry, droughty spots. As a result your personal landscape will be adapted to its natural environment and require far less time, energy, and resources to maintain it.

"Xeriscaping" — Gardening with Less Water. Xeriscaping is a new gardening and landscape approach gaining popularity in the West as it becomes painfully obvious that water is an ever more scarce and expensive resource. The term "xeriscaping" is derived from the Greek word *xeros* meaning "dry," and is applied to techniques that reduce the water required to maintain gardens. The xeriscaping movement had its birth in the Denver area in the early 1980s. It gathered momentum later in the decade as an increasing number of cities enacted ordinances requiring water-conserving landscaping for new industrial, commercial, and residential developments.

Xeriscaping stresses the establishment of landscapes adapted to the dry environments around them, rather than trying to transplant and maintain water-consumptive landscapes from the humid East or tropics. Included among the several techniques used to create water-thrifty gardens and landscapes are: reducing the areas devoted to lawns, planting water-conserving plants, using mulches where possible to conserve water, using soil amendments to increase the water-holding capacity of soils, grouping plants with similar water requirements close together, and, if absolutely needed, installing micro-irrigation systems that most efficiently meet the plants' water needs. Adopting these techniques can lead to a 30 to 80 percent reduction in water use compared to a "humid" gardening approach.

In designing a xeriscape take advantage of the water draining from roofs, driveways, and impervious surfaces for supplemental irrigation. Also consider planting species with greater water needs in swales and depressions that collect rainwater at the beginning of the dry season. Even water-conserving species may need additional irrigation, but once established they should require only natural rainfall.

Native plants play a natural role in western xeriscapes, since they, above all species, are adapted to the local environment. The wildflowers presented in the section on foothill species (page 141) are obvious candidates for water-conserving landscapes; however, alpine species like sulfur-flowered eriogonum and montane species like scarlet gilia are also quite drought tolerant. Trees, such as ponderosa pine, and shrubs, such as sagebrush (*Artemesia tridentata*), golden currant (*Ribies odoratum*, *R. aureum*), mountain mahogany (*Cercocarpus montanus*), and Woods's rose (*Rosa woodsii*), can also be used quite effectively in xeriscapes. Be sure to prune shrubs periodically so that they remain a manageable size, old wood is removed, and new vigorous growth is encouraged.

Further information about xeriscaping is available from the Agricultural Extension Service, city or regional water authorities, botanic gardens, or the Xeriscaping Council, Inc., the address of which appears in Appendix C.

Seaside Gardens. Some plants are difficult to grow in gardens exposed to fog and salt-laden winds coming off the Pacific Ocean. Many species of wildflowers, however, thrive in coastal areas and are naturally successful additions

Wildflowers for Xeriscaping

Blanketflower
Blue flax
Harebell
Mexican hat
Mule's ears
Pearly everlasting
Platte River penstemon
Rocky Mountain beeplant
Rocky Mountain penstemon
Scarlet gilia
Sulfur-flowered eriogonum
Tufted evening primrose

Rock garden.

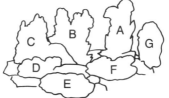

A. Sky pilot
B. Rocky Mountain penste-
   mon
C. Checker bloom
D. Bitterroot
E. Old-man-of-the-mountain
F. Mountain dryas
G. Harebell

to the seaside garden. Checker bloom, western bleeding hearts, and farewell-to-spring, with their masses of pink flowers, grow very well near the seaside, as do pearly everlasting, giant trillium, and giant evening primrose. Oregon grape (*Mahonia repens*), which is highly sensitive to salt, should not be planted along the immediate coast, but its close, salt-resistant relative *Mahonia pinnata* is a good alternative.

Meadows. Wildflower meadows are becoming increasingly popular alternatives to lawns, and western North American natives such as harebell, farewell-to-spring, pearly everlasting, blanketflower, Mexican hat, blue flax, and mule's ears can fill open spaces with color from late winter to early summer. Native wildflower meadows cost less than lawns to maintain, and consume less water, gasoline, fertilizers, and time.

The easiest time to create a wildflower meadow is when the land is bare and you do not have to deal with established, competing grasses, weeds, herbaceous plants, and woody seedlings. Meadow seeds can be purchased from many of the suppliers listed in Appendix A. If you are planning to plant a large area, you should inquire about wholesale prices for wildflower and native grass seed. And if you purchase formulated wildflower-grass seed mixtures, be sure they contain only those native species you really want in your meadow.

Natural valley grasslands and coastal prairies in this region (see page 6) are a combination of wildflowers and grasses. When planning your wildflower meadow select the grasses with great care. The chart below lists native grasses suitable for northwestern meadows. Some of these grasses are "cool-season" grasses that grow in the winter and spring in response to seasonal rains and then dry out and go into dormancy during the summer. The meadow grasses you interplant with the wildflowers should be bunch grasses — species that grow in clumps. Their shoots will provide support and the ideal amount of competition to enable the wildflowers to grow straight and tall. Avoid planting ryegrasses or bluegrasses which form a sod turf and crowd out the wildflowers.

Native wildflower seeds should be combined with a mixture of native grasses such as tufted hairgrass, blue grama, and western wheatgrass, with 60 to 90 percent of the seeds being grasses. The wildflower and grass seed mixture should be sown at a rate of 5 to 20 pounds of live seeds per acre, depending on the species composition. If species with small seeds make up the bulk of the seeds,

Native Western Grasses

COMMON NAME	LATIN NAME	HEIGHT	COMMENTS
Western wheatgrass	*Agropyron smithii*	12–24"	Tolerates both heat and cold; can be mown for a tolerable lawn.
Little bluestem	*Andropogon scoparius*	20–60"	Very attractive purple and orange stems when in fruit; fluffy fruits; good on dry soils.
Sideoats grama	*Bouteloua curtipendula*	24"	Good drought resistance and erosion control; excellent for desert meadows; can be mown as a lawn.
Blue grama	*Bouteloua gracilis*	15"	Very attractive seed heads; **very low water use**; sow in fall; can be mown to 1½ inch; good in mountains.
Buffalo grass	*Buchloe dactyloides*	2–5"	Low growing, can use as lawn; **very drought resistant**; spreads by runners; gray-green foliage.
California oatgrass	*Danthonia californica*	15–30"	Attractive open fruit heads; needs relatively well-drained, but moist soil.
Tufted hairgrass	*Deschampsia caespitosa*	8"	Hardy, lush foliage; can be mown as a lawn; good in mountains.
Sheep fescue	*Festuca ovina*	12"	Soft, narrow, blue-gray tufts; somewhat fragile, but withstands light shade.
June grass	*Koeleria cristata*	6–24"	Rocky Mountain bunchgrass; grows well on dry soil; flattened spikelets.
Indian ricegrass	*Oryzopsis hymenoides*	20"	Excellent for meadows or rock gardens; has attractive flowers that can be dried for arrangements; seeds are edible; drought resistant.
Pine bluegrass	*Poa scabrella*	12–30"	Native bunch grass that grows from coast to timberline; summer dormant at low elevations, remains green in mountains.
Porcupinegrass	*Stipa spartea*	24–40"	Rocky Mt. cool season grass; long, sharp-pointed fruits.

the seeding rate should be lower than with species with large, heavy seeds. The supplier from whom you purchase wildflower and grass seed in bulk can make specific seeding rate recommendations, but typically 6 to 7 pounds of wildflower seeds are mixed with enough grass seeds to sow an acre.

In the West it is best to sow the seeds either in autumn before the rains and snowy season or in the early spring just as soon as the soil can be worked. Choose a time when there will be sufficient moisture for the next 3 warm months to give the grass and wildflower seedlings an opportunity to become established. Do not plant the meadow when it is in full flower, since the seedlings will not have enough time to become established before summer, when heat and droughty conditions may make it difficult for seeds to germinate and seedlings to survive. In the Pacific Northwest coastal area early spring is an ideal time to plant meadows, while in montane areas fall plantings are usually more successful than spring plantings.

Sow the seeds on a windless day, broadcasting them by hand or using a whirlwind seeder. Keep the soil moist, but not wet, until the seeds have germinated, seedlings start to become established, and the rains have arrived. A light covering of seed-free straw will help to conserve moisture and reduce erosion until the meadow is established. Do not, however, use baled field hay, which is likely to contain the seeds of exotic grasses, species you want to prevent from invading your meadow.

A. June grass
B. Tufted hairgrass
C. Blanketflower
D. Harebell
E. Farewell-to-spring
F. Blue flax
G. Pearly everlasting
H. Mule's ears
I. Mexican hat
J. Western wheatgrass
K. Indian ricegrass

Wildflower meadow.

Transforming an Existing Field. More commonly, you are confronted with an existing lawn or field that you want to convert to a wildflower meadow. *Resist the impulse to use herbicides or fumigants to kill the existing vegetation.* Herbicides are likely to create more problems for the wildflower enthusiast than they solve. Apart from the damage they cause to the environment, they are not likely to save you any time in establishing a wildflower meadow. Hand weeding may take longer than spraying herbicide, but it is much safer.

One way to turn an existing field into a wildflower meadow is to start on a small scale by clearing small patches or strips in the fall, sowing native annual wildflowers and grasses, and transplanting live perennials the next spring, rather than just scattering seeds among established grasses. An even more successful approach for western meadows is to start perennial grass and wildflower plugs (see page 54) a year ahead and then to prepare the site a spring in advance, before the existing, unwanted field plants produce seeds.

Make patches by turning over sections of the field with a sharp spade or a rototiller. The patches should be 3 to 8 feet in diameter and dug in a random pattern, to create a more natural effect. If you prefer a border effect, clear strips in the field with a rototiller. Remove as many of the existing grass roots as possible, and water the soil to encourage the germination of any weed seeds that you have inadvertently stirred up in the process. Then cover the patch with heavy gauge black plastic sheet "mulch," pieces of discarded carpet, or even thick sections of newspaper. If you do not care for the sight of such coverings, you can spread a layer of bark mulch or soil on top of them. The covering will eventually shade out and kill off the remaining clumps of grass and the newly germinated weed seedlings.

Remove the coverings in mid-autumn before the rainy season begins. If black plastic mulch or carpet sections have been used, you may be able to use them again. Just place them where you intend to create the next year's patches.

Now plant the grass plugs in the patch, spacing them 12 to 15 inches apart. Transplant perennial native plants in between the clumps of grasses, and sow the seeds of annual wildflowers. The meadow will benefit from watering until the winter rains come, as well as from a light mulching with seed-free straw to conserve moisture and reduce erosion.

If your meadow already has bunch grasses, and you do not care to introduce new grass species, wildflower plugs and sods can be planted directly into the field in late autumn. Clear a small patch about a foot in diameter with a cultivator and pick out the grass roots. Set the live plants so the bases of their shoots are at the ground level. Press them down firmly so the roots are in good contact with the soil beneath, and water them.

Wildflower Meadow Maintenance. Repeat the steps each year until you are satisfied with your wildflower and native grass meadow. It may be a slow process, but even in nature a beautiful wildflower meadow, resplendent with a high diversity of desirable plants, is rarely produced in a single year.

Once the wildflower meadow is established it is relatively easy to maintain. Mow the meadow once a year with a rotary mower after the seeds have set. Grasslands are naturally swept by periodic fires. Meadows can be maintained by controlled burning, which kills many invading weed, shrub, and tree seedlings. Do not burn a meadow until after the second season, but then you can burn it every two to three years. Meadows are best burned on windless days, when the dormant grass is dry but the soil is still wet. If the meadow grass is too thin to support the fire, dry straw can be scattered about and ignited. *Be certain to observe local, state, and federal regulations concerning outdoor burning, in addition to the usual safety practices.* Check with your local fire department for assistance in planning any controlled burns and to obtain an outdoor burning permit.

In some suburbs there are ordinances dictating aesthetic standards for landscaping. If you live in such a community you might want to check with your city hall before converting your front yard into a prairie. If there are prohibitions, you can always try to get the law changed to encourage the landscaping use of native plants. Native plants are rarely the "weeds" that these ordinances are trying to prohibit, and it is unlikely that your blanketflowers or blue flax are going to march through your neighbor's water-consuming Kentucky bluegrass.

Plant Descriptions

The technical terminology used in the descriptions of the flowers, leaves, shoots, and roots for the species in this book has been kept to a minimum. The knowledge of some botanical terms is essential, however, and relatively painless to acquire.

FLOWERS Illustrated below are two typical flowers with all the parts that are usually present. *Complete flowers* have all the parts illustrated, but some of the wildflowers in the book lack one or more of the parts or they may be fused together in different arrangements. The trillium (below left) is a *simple flower*. The tidy tips (below right) is a *composite flower*.

In simple flowers, the flower parts are attached to a fleshy pad (the receptacle) atop the flower stem or *peduncle*. The outermost parts of the flower are the *sepals*, which are usually small, green, leaflike structures that cover and protect the flower while it is in the bud. Collectively, all of the sepals are called the *calyx*, Latin for "cup." In some species the sepals are fused together to form

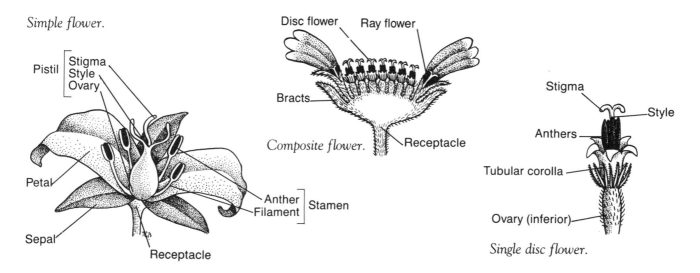

Simple flower.

Pistil { Stigma Style Ovary }

Petal

Sepal

Receptacle

Anther Filament } Stamen

Disc flower   Ray flower

Bracts

Composite flower.

Receptacle

Stigma

Style

Anthers

Tubular corolla

Ovary (inferior)

Single disc flower.

a tubular calyx, and in other species they resemble petals. Immediately inside the sepals are the *petals*, which may take on a variety of forms, some species having petals fused together into a tube, and others having petals that are free and unattached. On some flowers the petal arrangement is radially symmetrical, but on others, the petals take irregular forms. Collectively the petals are called the *corolla*, which means "small crown" in Latin.

In the center of the flower are the sexual parts, the male *stamens* and the female *pistil*. There may be one or several pistils, depending upon the species, but most flowering plants have more than one stamen. The stamen consists of a slender stalk, the *filament*, to which the pollen-bearing sacks, the *anthers*, are attached. The pistil has three major parts whose shapes may vary widely among species. The upper surface of the pistil, which receives pollen grains, is the *stigma*. The stigma is attached to the *ovary* at the base of the pistil by a usually slender tissue known as the *style*. Inside the ovary is a chamber containing the *ovules*, the female sex cells. After the pollen grains are deposited on the stigma, they germinate, sending microscopic tubes down through the style, through portions of the ovary, and finally into the ovules. Following fertilization, the ovules mature into *seeds*, and the ovary matures into the *fruit* of the plant.

The flowers of plants in the aster family, such as blanketflower and tidy tips, have a more complex structure. These species usually have two types of small flowers clustered together in a composite *flower head*. The small flowers or *florets* share a broad receptacle which is usually enclosed from below by many leafy bracts. The *ray flowers* usually form a ring around the outside of the head. Each ray flower has a relatively long, straplike petal which upon close inspection can be seen to be several small petals fused together. Often ray flowers are sterile and lack stamens and pistils entirely. In the center of the flower head are the even smaller *disc flowers*, with minute, tubular corollas. The stamens and the pistils in these flowers are surrounded by the petals, but are usually so small that magnification is required to see them clearly.

COLOR AND HEIGHT

Color of the flower and height of the plant are the gardener's first two concerns in deciding what species to plant. To aid in planning, the 33 species of plants described in this book are listed on page 31 by flower color and on page 32 by height. Use the information in these charts as a rough guide only. Keep in mind that some species, such as giant trillium, can appear in a range of colors. Also, the height of the plant depends on the environmental conditions in which it is grown. Further information concerning flower color and plant height is given in the descriptions of individual species.

FLOWER COLOR

SPECIES	PAGE	BROWN	WHITE	PINK	RED	ORANGE	YELLOW	GREEN	BLUE	PURPLE	LAVENDER
Giant trillium	100	●	●	●	●			●			
Bunchberry	110		●								
Mountain dryas	130		●								
Tufted evening primrose	150		●								
Solomon's seal	98		●								
Redwood sorrel	94		●	●							
Pearly everlasting	106		●				●				
Bitterroot	114		●—	—●							
Farewell-to-spring	84		●—	—●—	—●						●
Fireweed	112			●—	—●					●—	—●
Checker bloom	96			●							
Western bleeding hearts	86			●							
Elephantheads	136			●—	—●						
Rocky Mtn. beeplant	142			●							●
Scarlet gilia	146			●—	—●						
Leopard lily	88				●—	—●					
Blanketflower	144				●	●	●				
Mexican hat	152				●		●				
Sulfur-flowered eriogonum	132						●				
Yellow fawn lily	116						●				
Oregon grape	118						●				
Giant evening primrose	92						●				
Old-man-of-the-mountain	134						●				
Mule's ears	154						●				
Colorado columbine	108		●						●		
Washington lupine	90		●						●—	—●	
Blue flax	148								●		
Sky pilot	138								●		
Harebell	128								●		
Platte River penstemon	122								●—	—●	
Mountain bluebells	120								●		●
Rocky Mtn. penstemon	124								●—	—●	
Western Monkshood	104									●	

PLANT HEIGHT

Species	Page	Approx. height range (from bar chart)
Redwood sorrel	94	~1/4'
Old-man-of-the-mountain	134	~1/4'–1/2'
Bitterroot	114	~1/4'–3/4'
Tufted evening primrose	150	~1/4'–3/4'
Bunchberry	110	~1/4'–1'
Mountain dryas	130	~1/4'–1'
Sky pilot	138	~1/4'–1 1/2'
Harebell	128	~1/4'–3'
Oregon grape	118	~1/2'–1'
Elephantheads	136	~1/2'–2'
Checker bloom	96	~1/3'–1'
Western bleeding hearts	86	~3/4'–1 1/4'
Sulfur-flowered eriogonum	132	~3/4'–1 1/2'
Pearly everlasting	106	~3/4'–1 3/4'
Yellow fawn lily	116	~3/4'–2'
Giant trillium	100	~1'–1 1/2'
Mule's ears	154	~1'–2'
Platte River penstemon	122	~1'–2'
Scarlet gilia	146	~1'–2 1/2'
Rocky Mtn. penstemon	124	~1'–2 1/2'
Blue flax	148	~1'–3'
Colorado columbine	108	~1'–3'
Western bluebells	120	~1'–3'
Western Solomon's seal	98	~1'–3'
Farewell-to-spring	84	~1'–3'
Rocky Mtn. beeplant	142	~1 1/2'–3'
Mexican hat	152	~1 1/2'–3'
Leopard lily	88	~1 1/2'–3'
Washington lupine	90	~1 1/2'–4'
Blanketflower	144	~2'–3'
Western monkshood	104	~2'–5'
Fireweed	112	~2'–5'
Giant evening primrose	92	~3'–4'

Scale: 0' 1/2' 1' 2' 3' 4' 5' 10' 15'

FRUITS AND SEEDS

Fruits are as intriguing and varied as the flowers that produce them. The main function of fruits, which are formed from ripened ovaries, is to aid in the dissemination of the seeds they contain. The structure of various fruits often gives clues about how the seeds are disseminated. Many species that inhabit open spaces, like fireweed, mountain dryas, and pearly everlasting, depend upon the wind to carry their seeds away from the parent plants and often have light seeds with tufts of hairs to keep them buoyed by air currents.

Other wildflowers use different devices to disseminate their seeds. As the long stems of Colorado columbine wave in the wind, for example, the seeds are flung out of openings in the tops of the capsule fruits. The fleshy fruits of western Solomon's seal, Oregon grape, and bunchberry are eaten by various birds and mammals, and the seeds are then dropped after travelling through their digestive systems. Western bleeding hearts seeds have small, oily bodies known as "elaiosomes" attached to their surfaces. Ants find the elaiosomes irresistible, and carry the seeds off, chew off the elaiosome, and discard the seeds some distance from the parent plants. The seeds chewed upon by ants usually germinate better than those the ants have missed.

ROOT SYSTEMS

The forms of the underground portions of the 33 wildflowers described in this book vary greatly and may influence the types of habitats in which they can be grown. The root system also affects how easily a plant can be propagated. Six of the eight most common "root types" illustrated on page 34 are actually the underground stems, or "rootstocks," of perennials. The remaining two are true roots and lack leaf buds.

True Roots. True roots (illustrated on page 34) may be either diffuse and fibrous, as with many garden plants like western shooting star and blue-eyed grass, or they may be a strongly vertical, carrotlike *tap root* as with bitterroot and checker bloom. The root systems of some wildflowers are intermediate between the two basic types.

Runners and Stolons. Underground stems take a variety of forms. The simplest rootstock has thin horizontal branches, which give rise to new plants. These branches are usually called *runners* if they are above ground, as with strawberries, and *stolons* if they are below ground, as with mint and bunchberry.

Tubers. If the tip of a stolon produces a swollen, fleshy storage organ, it is called a *tuber*. The leaf buds of tubers are frequently called "eyes." The potato is probably the most familiar example of a tuber, but wildflowers such as western bleeding heart also have tuberous roots.

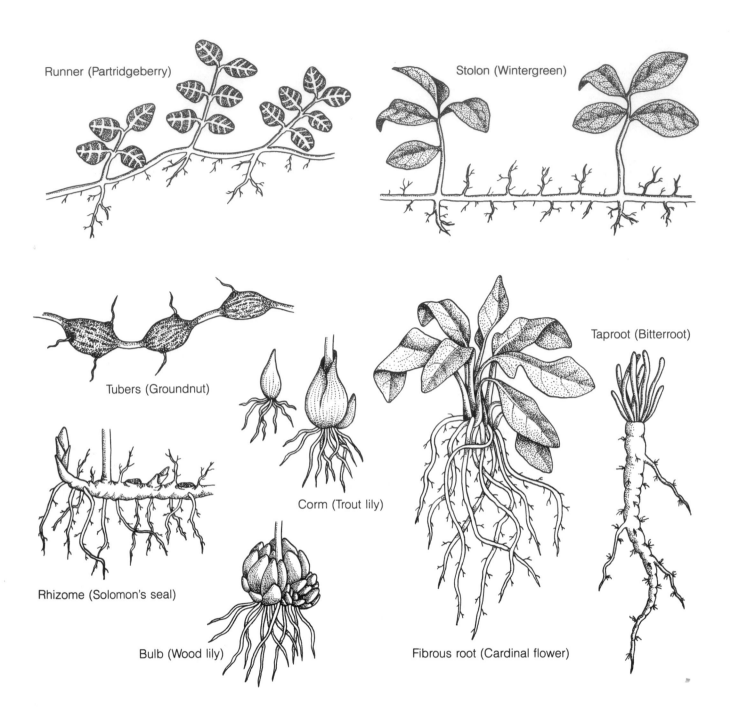

Runner (Partridgeberry)

Stolon (Wintergreen)

Tubers (Groundnut)

Taproot (Bitterroot)

Corm (Trout lily)

Rhizome (Solomon's seal)

Bulb (Wood lily)

Fibrous root (Cardinal flower)

Rhizomes. Thick, fleshy, horizontal underground stems with buds on their top surfaces and roots on their bottom surfaces are called *rhizomes*. Rhizomes, like those of western Solomon's seal and fireweed store large amounts of starch, which is used to nourish the shoots and flowers of perennials as they emerge from dormancy.

Corms and Bulbs. Rootstocks may also be round and bulbous. A true *bulb* is a bud atop a very short stem, surrounded by fleshy leaf scales, as with onions and leopard lily. *Corms* look like bulbs but are rootstocks formed from the swollen, solid base of the stem, as with gladiolus and giant trillium.

Flowering Season

A great number of factors, some genetic and some environmental, affect the onset and length of the flowering season of wildflowers. Complex interactions among climatic factors such as amount of sunlight, length of day, moisture, and temperature of air and soil influence exactly when plants start flowering.

Annual species usually have longer flowering seasons than perennials do and, of course, flower in a single growing season. Annuals may become persistent, even to the point of being considered weeds, through self-seeding. Perennials, on the other hand, may require several or many years to reach maturity and flower, but once established they generally require little maintenance, and reliably reappear year after year.

CLIMATE The overall climatic patterns of temperature and precipitation have a considerable effect on the blooming of wildflowers. In general, coastal areas, with the moderating effects of the Pacific Ocean, have more constant temperatures, more reliable precipitation, and longer growing seasons than do inland sites.

Precipitation and temperature are critical, influencing the timing of germination, the renewal of perennial growth, and the abundance of wildflowers. In years when the winter rains are erratic or far below average, especially if it is also unusually cold, springtime flowering may be delayed. On the other hand, if the rainy season precipitation is well distributed and temperatures are slightly above average, flowering may be accelerated.

Even though exact flowering times frequently vary, the flowering order of wildflower species within the same geographic area tends to be consistent from year to year. The general seasonal progression of flowering of the wildflowers in this book is shown on page 36. The seasons of flowering are given, rather than calendar months, because the onset of the growing season varies from locale to locale and from year to year. The seasons refer to the flowering of a given species near the center of its native range, and the gardener may find that the flowering sequence may be slightly different for plants obtained from different areas.

FLOWERING PROGRESSION

Species	Page	Late Winter	Early Spring	Midspring	Late Spring	Early Summer	Summer	Late Summer	Early Fall	Fall
Checker bloom	96		█							
Bitterroot	114		█	█						
Giant trillium	100		█	█						
Yellow fawn lily	116		█	█	█	█				
Redwood sorrel	94		█	█	█	█	█	█		
Giant evening primrose	92		█	█	█	█	█	█	█	
Oregon grape	118			█	█	█				
Mule's ears	154			█	█	█	█			
Sky pilot	138			█	█	█	█			
Washington lupine	90			█	█	█	█			
Western Solomon's seal	98				█					
Farewell-to-spring	84				█	█				
Tufted evening primrose	150				█	█	█			
Platte River penstemon	122				█					
Bunchberry	110				█					
Rocky Mtn. penstemon	124				█					
Colorado columbine	108				█	█				
Mountain bluebells	120				█	█				
Blue flax	148				█	█	█			
Mexican hat	152				█	█	█	█		
Mountain dryas	130					█				
Harebell	128					█	█	█		
Elephantheads	136						█			
Old-man-of-the-mountain	134						█			
Sulfur-flowered eriogonum	132						█			
Scarlet gilia	146						█			
Leopard lily	88						█			
Western monkshood	104						█	█		
Fireweed	112						█	█		
Western bleeding hearts	86						█	█		
Rocky Mtn. beeplant	142							█	█	
Blanketflower	144							█	█	█
Pearly everlasting	106							█	█	

LOCAL CONDITIONS

The exact time of flowering in your garden may also be influenced by local conditions such as slope, elevation, soil type, and mulches. If your garden slopes to the south, it will be warmer and spring will arrive sooner than if it slopes to the north. The warmest slopes are those on which the sun's rays strike most perpendicularly, but even a 5-degree south-facing slope may have a microclimate equivalent to that of a flat surface 300 miles farther south. A similar slope facing north would be correspondingly cooler. A garden located at the base of a mountain or a hill, on the other hand, may be chilled by the downslope settling of cold air, especially in the spring and fall. Flowering dates may vary by as much as several weeks, therefore, depending on the local topography.

The elevation of a garden will also influence how rapidly spring arrives. At a given latitude air temperatures generally decrease 3 degrees F per 1,000 feet of rise. For each 100-foot increase in elevation, the air temperature is only three-tenths of a degree cooler, but flowering is delayed by about one day. For example, it is possible in June to drive from Denver, Colorado (elevation 5,280 feet) to Mount Evans (elevation 14,264 feet), and travel in 30 miles from the heat of the Great Plains to alpine snowfields.

Proximity to the ocean, especially during the late spring and early summer fog season, may influence how rapidly plants grow and flower. It is not uncommon for coastal sites enshrouded in fog to be 20 degrees F or more cooler than areas several miles away. Onshore winds will also tend to reduce air temperatures during the spring and summer.

Soil conditions may advance or retard the progression of flowering. Sandy soils generally warm up more rapidly in the spring than do peaty or clayey soils. Dark-colored soils will warm more rapidly than light-colored soils will. Heavy mulches, while reducing frost and keeping soils warmer in the winter, provide an insulation layer that may both slow warming in the spring and maintain cooler soils in the summer.

GENETIC FACTORS

Some plants, but not all, are genetically programmed to flower in response to specific day lengths or hours of darkness. This characteristic is found in a wide variety of wildflowers, including annuals, biennials, and perennials. Some plants, such as western Solomon's seal, start to grow in the early spring and then flower most abundantly when days lengthen and nights become short. They are known as "long-day" plants, although they are actually responding to the short nights associated with late spring and early summer. The northern regions of North America, with relatively longer spring and summer day lengths, have a greater proportion of long-day plants than do southern regions. In fact, day length determines the southern limits of some long-day species.

Other species, such as the pearly everlasting, are "short-day" plants and flower when days are short and nights are long. These species are stimulated to flower by the long nights of late summer and fall.

Regional differences in climatic patterns and day lengths have led to the evolution of genetically distinct varieties in some wildflower species. Known as "ecotypes," these varieties are well adapted to local conditions. When individuals of different ecotypes are planted together in the same garden, they frequently will flower at different times.

EXTENDING THE FLOWERING SEASON

There are several ways in which the flowering season can be prolonged. The easiest way to extend the flower season of annual wildflowers is to make successive plantings at three-to-four-week intervals from the beginning of the rainy season to late winter. Some of the late sowings may not bear flowers, but there will still be blooms long after the flowers of the first sowing have withered. Some wildflowers will bloom longer if additional water is provided during the dry season, while others will simply rot. Consult the cultural requirements for individual wildflowers presented in Part III.

With species like scarlet gilia, trim some of the plants just before they set flower buds. That will delay their flowering by several weeks, and the clipped plants will come into bloom as the flowers on the untrimmed plants are fading. Many species, both annuals and perennials, will bloom longer if the fading flowers are removed ("deadheaded") before the fruits and seeds start to mature. The only drawback of this technique is that you sacrifice production of seed that could be used for further propagation.

If you have a number of different garden sites with varying slopes and exposures, the differences in microclimates may be sufficient to accelerate flowering in some plants and delay it in others. Another way to extend the flowering season of a given species is to purchase seeds or plants from suppliers in various geographic regions, so that different ecotypes are represented in the garden. The differences in their flowering times may be sufficient to prolong the season even of those species with short-lived flowers.

Wildflower Culture

LIGHT
CONDITIONS

While the vast majority of domesticated horticultural species planted in the garden require full sunlight for optimum growth, native plants have evolved to survive in a wide variety of light conditions, from full sun to shade. Therein lies an opportunity in gardening with wildflowers. The light preferences of the 33 species of native plants included in this book are given on page 40.

While some species are successfully grown only in a rather restricted range of light conditions, others can be cultivated in either sun or shade. The form of the plant often changes when grown under different light conditions. Typically when a plant is grown in the shade its leaves are thinner and larger and its stems are more spindly or "leggy" than when it is grown in the open. Some species, such as redwood sorrel, are so adapted to shade that they suffer leaf scorching if they have prolonged exposure to full sun on dry sites. Western Solomon's seal can withstand deep shade, but can be grown in full sun if sufficient water is provided.

TEMPERATURE

Most gardeners are familiar with hardiness zones, which indicate the relative mildness or severity of winter temperatures. (See page 42, U.S.D.A. Hardiness Zone Map.) The higher the hardiness zone number, the milder the winter climate. There is a great deal of similarity between hardiness zones and the length of the frost-free season (see map on page 61). Hardiness zones are based only on the average annual minimum winter temperature, however, and the frost-free season is the average length of time between the last killing frost in the spring and the first frost in the autumn. As you move from southern coastal to northern interior regions of northwestern North America, you will generally encounter shorter frost-free seasons and lower hardiness zone numbers, but this pattern is by no means uniform. The Pacific Coast has a significantly milder winter and a longer growing season than do the peaks of the Coast Ranges, the Sierra Nevada, the Rockies, or the high-elevation inland plateaus at the same latitude.

LIGHT CONDITIONS

Species	Page	Open / Full Sun	Filtered Sun / Partial Shade	Light Shade	Heavy Shade
Pearly everlasting	106	■			
Rocky Mtn. beeplant	142	■			
Mountain dryas	130	■			
Sulfur-flowered eriogonum	132	■			
Blanketflower	144	■			
Old-man-of-the-mountain	134	■			
Scarlet gilia	146	■			
Bitterroot	114	■			
Blue flax	148	■			
Tufted evening primrose	150	■			
Giant evening primrose	92	■			
Elephantheads	136	■			
Platte River penstemon	122	■			
Rocky Mtn. penstemon	124	■			
Sky pilot	138	■			
Mexican hat	152	■			
Mule's ears	154	■			
Western monkshood	104	■	■		
Harebell	128	■	■		
Farewell-to-spring	84	■	■		
Fireweed	112	■	■		
Yellow fawn lily	116	■	■		
Washington lupine	90	■	■		
Checker bloom	96	■	■		
Oregon grape	118	■	■		
Bunchberry	110	■	■	■	
Colorado columbine	108	■	■	■	
Western Solomon's seal	98	■	■	■	■
Leopard lily	88		■		
Mountain bluebells	120		■	■	
Western bleeding hearts	86		■	■	
Giant trillium	100		■	■	
Redwood sorrel	94		■	■	■

Species	Page	Open / Full Sun	Filtered Sun / Partial Shade	Light Shade	Heavy Shade

Most perennials have a limited range of hardiness zones in which they can survive. The approximate range of hardiness zones for the species of wildflowers in this book is given on page 42 and is shown on the individual range maps. The hardiness ranges indicated are approximate. You can usually cultivate perennials in colder areas if you insulate them with a heavy overwinter mulch to prevent frost penetration in the soil. Be careful to remove the mulch in the spring and to choose a mulching material that will not alter the desired acidity/alkalinity conditions for pH-sensitive species, as is explained in the section to follow concerning soils.

Many plants need chilling of their seeds as well. These seeds require or are enhanced by weeks or even months of exposure to temperatures of 40°F or below, to break their dormancy and germinate properly, as is discussed in the following section on propagation.

MOISTURE CONDITIONS

Just as wildflowers of the region have adapted to different temperature and light conditions, they have evolved to survive under different moisture conditions, ranging from the dry foothills of the Rockies to the rain forests of the Olympic Peninsula and the northern Pacific Coast. Precipitation in northwestern North America is generally abundant during the wet winter season, but can be scanty during the summer growing season when, typically, only 20 percent of the annual precipitation falls.

The geographic distribution of precipitation is far from uniform. Although precipitation generally decreases from the Coast to interior plateaus and the Rocky Mountains, the maximum precipitation is found near the summits of the Cascades and Sierra Nevada. Moisture-laden air masses, traveling inland from the Pacific Ocean, are forced to rise over these mountains, cooling and releasing snow or rain. The passage up the western slopes depletes the moisture from the air masses, which become warmer and even drier during their descent down the eastern slopes. The California Central Valley grassland is in the "rain shadow" of the Coast Ranges, and the Great Basin deserts are in the rain shadow of the Cascade and Sierra Nevada ranges (see the map on page 00). Precipitation again increases as air masses rise from the Great Basin and Columbia Plateaus passing toward the summits of the Rocky Mountains, only to decrease sharply again as they descend over the Great Plains on their eastward journeys. The relatively dry climate of the foothills east and west of the Rockies is a result of these rain-shadow effects.

On a local scale, the gardener should choose wildflowers adapted to the soil-moisture conditions that are present, as shown in the chart on page 44. Some

HARDINESS ZONES

Species	Page	1	2	3	4	5	6	7	8	9	10
Bunchberry	110	■	■	■	■	■	■				
Mountain dryas	130	■	■	■	■	■	■	■	■		
Blue flax	148	■	■	■	■	■	■	■	■	■	■
Elephantheads	136		■	■	■	■	■	■	■		
Western Solomon's seal	98		■	■	■	■	■	■	■		
Blanketflower	144		■	■	■	■	■	■	■		
Harebell	128		■	■	■	■	■	■	■	■	
Fireweed	112		■	■	■	■	■	■	■		
Platte River penstemon	122		■	■	■	■	■	■	■		
Pearly everlasting	106		■	■	■	■	■	■	■	■	■
Old-man-of-the-mountain	134			■	■	■					
Yellow fawn lily	116			■	■	■	■				
Colorado columbine	108			■	■	■	■	■			
Sulfur-flowered eriogonum	132			■	■	■	■	■			
Mountain bluebells	120			■	■	■	■	■	■		
Sky pilot	138			■	■	■	■	■	■		
Washington lupine	90			■	■	■	■	■	■	■	
Bitterroot	114			■	■	■	■	■	■	■	■
Rocky Mtn. penstemon	124				■	■	■	■	■		
Western monkshood	104				■	■	■	■	■		
Western bleeding hearts	86				■	■	■	■	■		
Scarlet gilia	146				■	■	■	■	■		
Leopard lily	88				■	■	■	■	■		
Tufted evening primrose	150				■	■	■	■	■		
Giant evening primrose	92				■	■	■	■	■	■	■
Mule's ears	154				■	■	■	■	■	■	
Oregon grape	118					■	■	■	■		
Mexican hat	152					■	■	■	■		
Giant trillium	100						■	■	■		
Redwood sorrel	94								■	■	
Checker bloom	96								■	■	■
Farewell-to-spring HA	84										
Rocky Mtn. beeplant HA	142										

Species	Page	1	2	3	4	5	6	7	8	9	10

HA (Hardy Annual): Seeds can withstand cold winter temperatures.

species, such as mountain bluebells, thrive in damp soils, yet can also be easily cultivated in well-drained soils of moderate moisture — conditions typical of most flower gardens. Many species need moisture while they are becoming established in the garden, but then grow better if the soils are not overly wet. Wildflower gardeners should be judicious with the hose; bitterroot, penstemons, and other species suffer from root rot or leaf mildews if they are kept too wet, and seedlings of most wildflowers are especially sensitive to fungal attack when soils are cold and wet.

Cultivating wildflowers is easiest when you match a species' optimal requirements with those naturally occurring in the garden, so consider your soil before selecting wildflowers. If your soil is sandy, it will probably drain quickly, and you should consider planting species that do well in drier conditions. Clayey and peaty soils are often poorly drained, making them hospitable to species preferring plenty of soil moisture during the rainy season, but they can become excessively dry during the remainder of the year.

If your soil conditions do not quite suit a particular species, however, you may be able to add the proper soil amendments before planting. A little extra time and energy invested in site preparation will pay large dividends in the future, so do not rush your wildflowers into soils to which they are ill adapted. Avoid merely piling soil amendments on top of the soil where they will have marginal effect; instead, work them thoroughly into the soil. Organic matter well mixed into the soil will aerate it and increase its water-holding capacity.

If your soil is too dry, the garden not too large, and your hose long enough, it is obviously easy to increase the soil moisture by watering. However, adding clay, compost, humus, or even coarse organic matter such as leaves may be a more effective way of assuring the long-term retention of moisture. Mulches are an integral part of xeriscaping in dry foothill regions because they reduce evaporation from the soil surface. They are excellent to use around the bases of perennials, but may prevent small seeded annual wildflowers from self-seeding.

If the soil is too wet during the rainy season because of an overabundance of clay, you can improve the drainage by adding sand or gravel mixed with copious amounts of compost or other organic matter. The organic matter creates additional air spaces in clayey soil and helps to prevent the clay from merely coating the grains of sand. Alternatively, gypsum (calcium sulfate) can be added to clayey soil to improve drainage. Since gypsum is an acidifying agent, it should be used where you will be planting wildflowers that thrive in acid soil, with a pH of 5.5 and below. Gypsum has the additional benefit of helping conserve nitrogen compounds in the soil. It is available at many garden or building-supply centers.

SOIL MOISTURE CONDITIONS

Species	Page	Wet	Damp	Moist	Moderately or Seasonally Dry	Arid
Elephantheads	136	■				
Redwood sorrel	94	■	■			
Bunchberry	110		■	■		
Mountain bluebells	120	■	■			
Western bleeding hearts	86			■		
Yellow fawn lily	116			■		
Leopard lily	88			■		
Western Solomon's seal	98			■		
Washington lupine	90			■	■	
Colorado columbine	108			■	■	
Giant evening primrose	92			■	■	
Checker bloom	96			■		
Western monkshood	104			■	■	
Giant trillium	100			■	■	
Old-man-of-the-mountain	134			■	■	
Fireweed	112			■	■	
Farewell-to-spring	84			■	■	
Platte River penstemon	122			■	■	
Rocky Mtn. penstemon	124			■	■	
Blanketflower	144			■	■	
Blue flax	148			■	■	
Mexican hat	152			■	■	
Mule's ears	154			■	■	
Pearly everlasting	106				■	
Harebell	128				■	
Rocky Mtn. beeplant	142				■	
Mountain dryas	130				■	
Sulfur-flowered eriogonum	132				■	
Scarlet gilia	146				■	
Oregon grape	118				■	
Sky pilot	138				■	
Tufted evening primrose	150				■	
Bitterroot	114				■	■

pH, SALINITY, AND OTHER SOIL CONDITIONS

The specific soil requirements of 33 native plants are given on the individual species description pages. Some species thrive where nutrient levels are high and humus is abundant in the soil. Other species do best where there is little organic matter and the soil fertility is low.

One of the most important conditions in the cultivation of many wildflowers is the *pH* of the soil. The pH is simply a measure of the relative acidity or alkalinity on a scale from 0 (most acidic) to 14 (most alkaline), with a value of 7 indicating neutral conditions. The pH units are based on multiples of ten, so that a soil with a pH of 4.0 is 10 times more acidic than a soil with a pH of 5.0, and 100 times more acidic than a soil with a pH of 6.0. Likewise, a pH of 9 is 10 times more alkaline than a pH of 8, and so forth.

The pH of the soil is important because it influences the availability of nutrients essential for plant growth. Nutrients such as phosphorus, calcium, potassium, and magnesium are most available to plants when the soil pH is between 6.0 and 7.5. Under highly acidic (low pH) conditions these nutrients become insoluble and relatively unavailable for uptake by plants. However, iron, trace minerals, and some toxic elements such as aluminum become *more* available at low pH. A major concern about acid rain is the possible increased absorption of these toxic elements by plants.

High soil pH may also decrease the availability of nutrients. If the soil is more alkaline than pH 8, phosphorus, iron, and many trace minerals become insoluble and unavailable for plant uptake.

The availability of nitrogen, one of plants' three key nutrients, is influenced by pH conditions as well. Much of the nitrogen that plants eventually use is bound within organic matter, and the conversion of this bound nitrogen to forms available to plants is accomplished by several species of bacteria living in the soil. When the soil's pH drops below 5.5, the activity of these bacteria is inhibited, and little nitrogen is available to the plants.

The usual pH range of soils is from about 4 to about 8. Over millennia, rocks and minerals decompose and slowly release large amounts of potassium, calcium, magnesium, and other alkaline nutrients. In humid areas of the Northwest ample rainfall has removed these elements from the soil. In the more arid areas of the West, however, intense evaporation and scanty rainfall have led to accumulation of these nutrients and the production of highly alkaline or saline soils in some locations. As a result the soils of the region show great variability, ranging from quite acidic to highly alkaline with pH values substantially above 7. Poorly designed or poorly operated irrigation systems further contribute to increased salinity in the West by bringing additional salts to the soil surface. In some low-lying basins salt deposits even encrust the surface of the soil, making the growth of most plants impossible.

Species	Page	pH range (approx.)
Fireweed	112	3.8 – 8.4
Bunchberry	110	4.0 – 5.0
Giant trillium	100	4.5 – 6.5
Redwood sorrel	94	4.5 – 6.8
Oregon grape	118	4.5 – 7.5
Checker bloom	96	4.5 – 7.7
Yellow fawn lily	116	5.0 – 6.5
Western Solomon's seal	98	5.0 – 6.5
Washington lupine	90	5.0 – 7.0
Blue flax	148	5.0 – 7.7
Mountain bluebells	120	5.3 – 7.0
Mountain dryas	130	5.3 – 7.6
Old-man-of-the-mountain	134	5.3 – 8.0
Leopard lily	88	6.0 – 7.0
Colorado columbine	108	6.0 – 8.0
Harebell	128	6.0 – 8.0
Western bleeding hearts	86	6.0 – 8.0
Mexican hat	152	6.0 – 8.0
Sulfur-flowered eriogonum	132	6.5 – 8.0
Western monkshood*	104	4.5 – 7.8
Pearly everlasting	106	4.5 – 7.8
Farewell-to-spring	84	4.5 – 7.8
Rocky Mtn. beeplant	142	4.5 – 7.8
Blanketflower	144	4.5 – 7.8
Scarlet gilia	146	4.5 – 7.8
Bitterroot	114	4.5 – 7.8
Tufted evening primrose	150	4.5 – 7.8
Giant evening primrose	92	4.5 – 7.8
Elephantheads	136	4.5 – 7.8
Platte River penstemon	122	4.5 – 7.8
Rocky Mtn. penstemon	124	4.5 – 7.8
Sky pilot	138	4.5 – 7.8
Mule's ears	154	4.5 – 7.8

pH scale across top and bottom: 3 4 5 6 7 8 9 10

*This and the following species appear to have no strong pH preferences.

Local soil acidity/alkalinity conditions may also vary because of differences in bedrock geology or vegetation. In general, limestone or marble bedrock produces mildly alkaline soils, and granite bedrock produces acidic soils.

In some places in the Coast Ranges there are outcrops of the lustrous gray-green mineral serpentine. Many species of domesticated and native plants grow very poorly, if at all, in serpentine areas, because the soil is deficient in calcium yet has an overabundance of magnesium and toxic metals such as nickel and cadmium. Heavy applications of ground limestone can overcome the lack of calcium and reduce the toxicity of metals in these soils.

Certain species of plants may also increase the acidity of the soil through the addition of organic matter with a low pH. Coniferous forests are noted for their acidic soils. The dead foliage of pines, spruce, fir, as well as oaks and heath plants, deposited on top of the soil, further acidifies the soil as it decomposes. In cool, wet areas, the growth of mosses may also create locally the acidic conditions typical of regions with needle-leaved forests.

Some species of wildflowers are relatively insensitive to soil acidity/alkalinity conditions, while others survive only over a narrow pH range. Most often pH preferences are related more to the balance of various nutrients required by particular species, or to changes in the biological activity of soil organisms, rather than to acidity or alkalinity itself. On page 46 is a guide to the pH preferences of those species of wildflowers that have specific soil pH requirements. It is often difficult to grow species close together if they have vastly different pH requirements. It is best to grow acid-loving species such as bunchberry in a different section of the garden than species that prefer alkaline soils.

HOW TO MEASURE pH

Before deciding which wildflowers to cultivate and where to plant them, it is essential to know something about the pH of your soils. The measurement is actually quite simple, and a number of commercial products are readily available from most garden suppliers. The pH is measured by taking samples of soil from the root zone at several different spots in the garden. Using a plastic spoon, place the soil in a small plastic or glass vial, and add an equal volume of water. Shake or stir the sample to mix the soil and water thoroughly, and allow the soil to settle. The pH of the liquid in the top of the vial can then be determined by any one of several means.

The least expensive way to measure pH is with "indicator paper," which can be purchased in short strips or long rolls. This is like litmus paper, but rather than merely showing you whether a solution is acid or alkaline, it produces a range of colors to indicate the pH value. Just stick the strip of paper into the liquid extracted from the soil and compare the color of the dampened paper to the reference chart provided.

A slightly more accurate method, although usually more expensive, is the use of indicator solutions, which are frequently sold in pH kits. A small amount of the liquid extracted from the soil-and-water mix is placed in a ceramic dish, and a few drops of indicator solution are added. As with the indicator papers, the color produced is compared to a pH reference chart.

You can also measure pH with a meter. One type of pH meter operates without batteries and measures pH based on the conductivity of the moistened soil. This type of pH meter is neither more accurate nor faster than the color-indicator methods that use solutions or paper. All provide a rough, but useful, estimate of soil pH.

The most accurate measurements of soil pH use electronic meters with one or several electrodes. These instruments are quite expensive and are used by soil-testing laboratories for determining soil pH. Most state Agricultural Experiment Stations, usually located at land-grant universities, will test soil samples for a nominal charge. To arrange for such pH testing, contact your state's land-grant university or your county's Agricultural Extension Service agent.

CHANGING THE pH OF SOILS

You may find that the pH of your soil does not suit a particular species, even though all other environmental conditions seem perfect. The acidity or alkalinity of soils can be altered to a limited extent through the addition of various soil amendments. It may take several years to change a soil's pH permanently, however, so be patient.

Pine, spruce, redwood, or fir needles can be added to garden soils to lower the pH. If none of these is locally available, peat moss also works well in acidifying soils. Powdered gypsum (calcium sulfate) or sulfur powder can be used to lower soil pH, but these should be used with caution, because they act more rapidly than do the organic materials.

Ground limestone is the amendment of choice to raise the pH of the soil. Medium-ground limestone may give better long-term results than very coarse limestone (which may be slow to neutralize soil acids) or very fine limestone (which may be lost too quickly from the soil). Wood ashes can also be used, but keep in mind that they are more concentrated than limestone and may even "burn" wildflowers if too much is applied.

After measuring the pH, add the soil amendment, taking care to mix thoroughly and incorporate it uniformly in the top 6 to 12 inches of soil. Spread the amendment thinly on the ground, and work it into the soil with a spading fork or shovel. Then add another layer, mixing it into the soil. If you do not mix the amendment evenly you may find pockets of soil with enormously different pH values. Moisten the soil, and then allow it to rest for a day or so before again measuring the pH at several spots. Repeat the process until you have the desired pH conditions.

A very rough rule of thumb is that for a 100-square-foot area of most soils it takes about 2 to 6 pounds of limestone to raise the pH one unit, and 2½ to 7 pounds of gypsum or ½ to 2 pounds of sulfur to lower the pH one unit. Clay soils require more of an amendment to change the pH; sandy soils, less.

It is strongly recommended that organic matter acidifiers be used before resorting to gypsum or sulfur. It is better to change the pH of the soil slowly than to overdo it one way and then the other.

After the appropriate pH is attained, check it periodically. Since the natural processes at work in your garden will be altering the pH through rainfall, bacterial activity, the uptake of nutrients by plants, and climatic factors, you may occasionally have to make further additions of soil amendments. With wildflowers in place, be especially careful to add the amendments in small amounts directly on the surface of the soil, and work them in with minimal disturbance of the plants' roots.

A WORD ABOUT WEEDS AND PESTS

Wildflowers growing in their natural habitats are obviously well adapted for survival under the prevailing local conditions. Gardening, however, involves disturbing the soil and modifying the moisture and, often, light conditions. These changes often invite unwelcome and unwanted plants — weeds.

Many of the worst weeds, such as Klamath weed or Saint Johnswort (*Hypericum perforatum*), mouse-ear chickweed (*Cerastium vulgatum*), field bindweed (*Convolvulus arvensis*), and dandelion (*Taraxacum officinale*), have their origins in Europe or Asia and have found a new home to their liking in the Northwest. In contrast to many of the desirable native wildflowers, weeds tend to grow quickly, spread aggressively, and set loose copious quantities of highly mobile seeds. Often weeds will accomplish these feats so quickly that they produce many generations in the time it takes to produce a single generation of desired wildflowers. The seeds of weeds tend to be long-lived and may remain dormant for many years, buried in the soil, just waiting for the proper conditions to germinate. Studies have shown that the seeds of some weeds can remain dormant yet capable of germinating for more than forty years. Typically, there are hundreds of weed seeds beneath each square yard of soil surface. Gardening activity frequently brings the weed seeds to the surface and provides ideal conditions for them to thrive.

Weeds are thus inevitable, but do not despair, and *do not resort to the use of herbicides!* Many wildflowers are particularly sensitive to the effects of herbicides, so weeding by hand is the only real choice. You will find that a modest investment of time spent weeding while your wildflowers are first becoming established will pay large dividends. Even natural gardens may need some weeding during the first several years. Once the plants are well established and holding their ground, weeds will have a more difficult time invading, and weeding will be less necessary.

You will find from time to time that various insects will visit your wildflowers, and while some of these may be there for an attractive meal, they usually have an abundance of natural predators that will keep their populations in check so that minimal damage occurs. Some wildflowers, like lupines, may look a bit tattered by the end of the season, because butterfly larvae have chewed holes in the leaves. Usually the plants have suffered little, and *the use of pesticides is unwarranted*, especially if you are trying to attract butterflies, bees, or even hummingbirds to the garden. The use of pesticides is also to be avoided because many wildflowers are pollinated by insects, and without the pollinators, there is no fruit and seed production. If aphids become a problem because their naturally occurring biological control agents are lacking, try controlling them with insecticidal soaps.

When establishing or maintaining a wildflower garden, slugs, household pets, ground squirrels, gophers, birds, and, in rural areas, deer may be more of a problem than insects are. Trapping and removal of gophers and ground squirrels may be necessary if you, your wildflowers, and these wildlife species cannot reach an accommodation. If dogs, cats, or deer become a nuisance, fencing may be the only reasonable solution. Large, robust seedlings that have been started in flats and transplanted may be more resistant to animal attack than are tender seedlings just emerging from the soil. Sometimes, what appears to be indiscriminate eating of wildflowers by mammals actually increases their growth. Scarlet gilia, for example, produces more flowers after being moderately grazed upon by deer and elk. If wildlife persist in decimating a particular species, however, try planting another, less enticing one.

Slugs and snails relish certain species of wildflowers, especially those in the lily family. They feed at night when the humidity is high, and can do considerable damage by chewing and stripping leaves. Slugs and snails can be easily and effectively controlled by hand picking, or if you find that approach offensive, by setting out dishes filled with stale beer. The shallow tubs in which whipped cream cheese or margarine are packaged make ideal traps. Make a "rain protector" for the trap by poking 3 holes in the lid in a triangular pattern and insert a plastic soda straw in each. Trim the straws so the lid rests an inch above the rim of the tub. Fill the tubs three-quarters full with beer and set them about the garden. The snails and slugs much prefer beer to your wildflowers, and once swimming in the brew they drown. Every several days, especially after heavy rains, you may have to dispose of the contents and replenish the beer.

Wildflower Propagation

One of the pleasures of growing wildflowers is the opportunity to propagate them and thereby increase their numbers in your garden. As has already been pointed out, digging wildflowers from their native environments is not only unethical, but also frequently illegal. The best way to obtain wildflowers for your garden is to purchase seeds, plants, or planting stock from reputable suppliers who sell nursery-propagated material (see Appendix A). Once your wildflowers are established, they can serve as stock for further propagation for your garden.

SEEDS Seeds are by far the cheapest way to propagate large numbers of wildflowers, even though some perennials grown from seeds may take a long time before they are mature enough to flower. Usually seeds are collected when the fruits are mature. Many species have seed dispersal mechanisms which may make it difficult to find plants with the fruits present when you want to harvest them. One way to capture the seeds before they are released from the plant is to cut a foot-long section of a discarded nylon stocking and make a sleeve, tying off one end with a string or twisted wire closure. Slip the sleeve over the developing fruit after the flower petals have withered, but before the fruit is fully ripe. Firmly but gently tie the open end closed so that the seeds can't fall to the ground, being careful not to crush or break the stem in the process. When the fruits are fully ripe, snip the stem just below the nylon bag, put it in a labeled paper sack, and bring it indoors for further processing.

Some seeds should be planted fresh and not allowed to dry out, or germination will be delayed. Other seeds will not germinate immediately and have to undergo a process of "after-ripening" before they are ready to sprout. Seeds of fleshy fruits should generally be separated from the pulp prior to storage or planting. If seeds are not the kind that need to be planted immediately and you desire to store them for a while, allow them to air-dry for several weeks and then separate the seeds from the dried remains of the fruit. Gently crushing the dried fruits on a large sheet of white paper will usually release the seeds, which should then be separated from the chaff. The chaff can be removed either by blowing gently across the paper or, if seeds are small enough, by sifting through a strainer. Store the cleaned seeds in small manila coin envelopes, zip-closure bags, or 35mm film canisters.

The seeds of some species will remain dormant unless they undergo certain specific treatments — chilling, scratching of their seed coats, exposure to light or darkness, heating by fire, or a combination of these treatments. The treatments required to germinate specific seeds are detailed on the descriptive pages following this chapter. These treatments fall into four categories: seed chilling, or *stratification*; seed-coat scratching, or *scarification*; heat treatments; light or dark treatment.

Stratification. Some plants that live in northwestern North America have evolved seeds that are dormant the first fall after they have been produced. This adaptation prevents tender seedlings from coming up and facing freezing temperatures when they would be only a month or so old. Breaking dormancy requires the seeds to be subjected to a period of cold temperatures (stratification), followed by a period of warm temperatures — as in the natural progression of seasons. Usually a temperature of only 40 degrees F is sufficient to break dormancy or enhance germination. The length of stratification varies widely among different species. Some seeds germinate more successfully if they are stratified under moist conditions in addition to the cold temperatures.

The easiest way to stratify seeds in the Northwest is to plant the seeds outdoors in the fall and let Nature do it for you. Seeds can be planted directly in the garden where desired or in flats that are left outdoors. If you do not desire to plant the seeds in the fall, place the container or envelope of seeds under refrigeration for the appropriate period of time. If moist stratification is required, the seeds can be placed in damp sphagnum moss or rolled up in lightly dampened paper towels and placed in an air-tight container or zip-closure plastic bag for the duration of the stratification.

Scarification. In order for seeds to germinate they have to take up water and oxygen from the outside environment through the outer covering of the seed, called the *seed coat*. Some native species, especially those in the bean family, have seed coats so tough that water and oxygen cannot enter. These seeds remain dormant until the seed coat is scratched, or scarified. This occurs naturally when seeds are moved around in the soil, especially following heavy rainstorms, but in the home garden better results are obtained if the seeds are scarified by the gardener before planting.

The easiest way to scarify medium-size seeds is to rub the seeds between two sheets of medium-grit sandpaper. You don't want to rub them so hard that you pulverize the seeds, just hard enough to scratch up the surface so that moisture can penetrate to the seed inside. Large seeds can be scarified by nicking the seed coat with a sharp pocket knife.

Heat Treatments. Some seeds germinate better after being submerged in hot water prior to planting. Place the seeds in a jar and fill it halfway with tap water that is hot to the touch, but not scalding. Allow the seeds to remain in the water as it cools overnight. The seeds can then be planted the next day.

Light or Dark Treatments. A few species of wildflowers have seeds that are either stimulated or inhibited by light. If the seeds are stimulated by light they should be planted shallowly, so sunlight penetrating through the surface of the soil can have its desired effect. If the seeds are inhibited by light, they should be planted at sufficient depth to prevent light from slowing germination.

PLANTING TECHNIQUES

One of the most efficient ways to propagate wildflowers from seed is to use flats or nursery beds for rearing seedlings for the first year or until they become established. The advantage of flats is that you can transplant seedlings to holding beds and maintain an optimum density of plants more easily than if you plant the seed directly in the desired location. Also, some species have seed that is slow to germinate, and it may take several years for all the viable seeds that were planted to produce seedlings. The soil can be kept in the flats until the seeds have had sufficient time to germinate completely.

If you have only a few seeds, small pots can be used for raising seedlings. If the species is one that thrives in slightly acidic conditions, peat pots are a real convenience. When the seedlings are sturdy they can be transplanted to a nursery bed, where they can grow without competition from other plants, or to permanent locations. Be careful not to disturb the roots or to break off the shoots when removing the seedlings and soil from pots. If you are using peat pots, simply tear off the bottom of the pot and plant the container with its contents so that the surface level of the soil is the same as that inside the pot. (Unlike many gardeners, I tear off the bottom of the peat pot, because I have found the plant makes better contact with the soil that way.)

Soil Mixes and Potting. The soil in which a seed germinates and the seedling starts out is every bit as important as that in which the adult plant grows. A potting soil should have both good drainage and good water-holding capacity. While commercially formulated starting mixes are available from home and garden centers, you can make an inexpensive but effective mix by adding one part milled sphagnum to one part washed builder's sand. The resulting mix is weed-free and sterile. One convenient way to start seeds is to use 4½-by-6¼-inch plastic flats that are 2½ inches deep. Fill the flat to the top with the potting mix and then tamp down the surface, with the bottom of another flat, so that the soil surface is just below the rim. Set the seeds on the soil surface, and then cover them with the appropriate depth of additional soil. Moisten the soil with a fine sprinkle, and cover the top of the flat with plastic wrap to help conserve soil moisture. Leave the plastic on the flats until the seeds germinate and the tops of the seedlings are just pushing against the film.

Plugs and Sods. An effective way to grow live plants for transplanting to meadows is to produce wildflower *plugs* and *sods*. Plugs are individual live plants that have been grown in small pots or special trays. They can be efficiently transplanted into meadows or gardens because of their compact, dense mass of roots. They are most easily produced in special plug trays available through greenhouse supply companies and larger garden centers. These trays have cavities up to 2 inches in diameter and 2 inches deep with gently tapering sides so that the plugs can be easily removed.

To produce wildflower plugs, use the larger trays with 2-inch openings, and fill the cavities with potting mix as you would other pots or flats. Allow the seedlings to develop until the roots fully bind the soil in the cavities, a process that may take most of a growing season for some species. Water the plugs by periodically setting the entire tray in a shallow pan and allowing the water to be drawn up from the bottom. The wildflowers can be transplanted into the garden or meadow when a gentle tug at the base of the plant's stem pulls the entire plug, soil and all, out of the cavity.

Wildflower sods are like plugs, only larger. Sods can be made with a number of different wildflowers and grasses grown densely together in flats. You then transplant the entire contents of the flat into a meadow or garden. One way to make sods easier to handle is to line the flat with cheesecloth before adding the potting soil. The seeds are then planted in the soil, and as the seedlings mature their roots will penetrate the cloth liner. When it is time to transplant the sod, you can lift it out of the flat by pulling on the cheesecloth. Once in the ground, the roots of the sod plants will quickly grow through the cheesecloth and after about a year the cloth will simply decompose.

A Special Note on Legumes. Members of the bean family often require the presence of special microorganisms, known as *rhizobia*, in the soil to ensure their survival. These microbes lead a symbiotic existence with these plants, inhabiting nodules formed on the root systems and producing nitrogen compounds that the plants eventually use. Not all soils have abundant populations of these necessary microbes. If you have difficulty in propagating leguminous wildflowers like lupines, you may need to purchase a commercially produced "inoculant" and add it to the soil when you plant the seeds. Different species require different strains of microbial inoculants, so the addition of "pea" or "soybean" inoculants would not necessarily be effective for wildflowers. Make sure you get the right strain of rhizobia for the species you plan to cultivate.

Rhizobia inoculants can be ordered directly from the *Nitragin Division of LiphaTech, Inc., 3101 W. Custer Avenue, Milwaukee, WI 53209*, or from *Kalo, Inc., P.O. Box 12567, Columbus, OH 43212*. You will need to indicate the scientific name of the species to be inoculated and the amount of seed you intend to treat. It may take two to four weeks for these companies to prepare special rhizobia if they are not in stock.

ROOTSTOCK DIVISIONS

One of the quickest ways to propagate perennials is by rootstock division. Rootstocks are best dug up and divided while the plant is dormant. In general, perennials that flower in the spring can be most successfully divided in the fall, and those that flower in the summer or fall are best divided in the early spring. For those species like bitterroot whose shoots wither and enter dormancy before the end of the growing season, the location of the plants should be marked with a stake so that the rootstocks can be found later in the fall for propagation.

Regardless of the type of rootstock (see illustration on page 34) the principal technique is quite similar (see illustration on page 56). With a sharp knife (a pocket knife will do splendidly), cut the rootstock so that the divided pieces have at least one vegetative bud or "eye" attached. Since the size of the resulting plant will be determined to a large extent by the size of the divided piece, don't make the divisions too small (unless you want lots of tiny plants).

Runners and stolons are easily divided by cutting the horizontal stem between adjacent rooted plants, which can then be dug up and transplanted when dormant. The division of tubers is also easily accomplished. Cut tubers into pieces, each with a bud or two, and plant them with the buds pointing up (the way you would plant pieces of potato). New shoots and roots will be produced as the plant draws upon the energy reserves of the tuber flesh. Rhizomes similarly can be divided into pieces, each with buds and associated roots. Replant the segments at the appropriate depth and spacing.

Corms and bulbs of perennial wildflowers can be divided in a manner similar to other garden perennials. The small offsets that develop on the sides of mature corms and bulbs can be removed with a knife during the dormant season and planted at the appropriate depth. These cormlets and bulblets will usually take several years to develop into plants capable of flowering. If not cut off the parent rootstock, these offsets eventually mature into large, densely crowded plants that will benefit from being divided and given wider spacing.

The fleshy scales of bulbs such as lilies can be divided and planted like seeds in flats to produce large quantities of "seedlings." Break off the individual scales from dormant bulbs, and in a flat containing potting soil mixture, plant them just below the soil surface, with the tips of the scales pointing upward. Provide light shade and keep the soil moist, but not overly wet, until the resulting small plants are sturdy enough to transplant into a nursery bed or permanent location.

After replanting the rootstock divisions be especially careful not to overwater the soil. Although the soil should be prevented from thoroughly drying out, wet soils may invite problems. Rootstocks have carbohydrate-rich stores of energy that the plant draws upon during its period of most rapid growth.

Rootstock propagation.

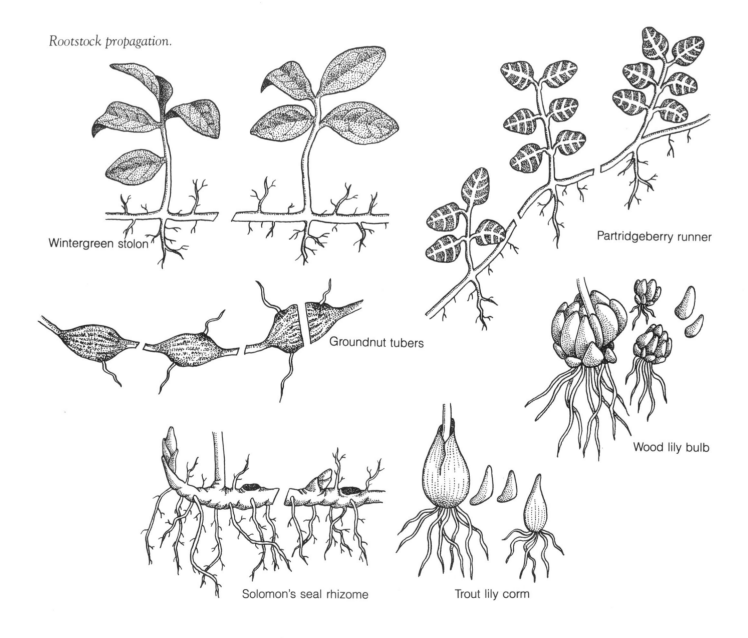

Wintergreen stolon

Partridgeberry runner

Groundnut tubers

Wood lily bulb

Solomon's seal rhizome

Trout lily corm

If the soil is too wet, bacterial and fungal rots may attack the newly divided rootstock pieces and even kill the plants. For this reason, it is a good idea to plant rootstock divisions in a nursery or holding bed that has well-drained soil, and to transplant the stock when dormant the following year.

STEM CUTTINGS Another successful way to propagate some perennials is to make cuttings of stems. These cuttings should be made when the shoots are growing vigorously and are most successful if the shoot lacks flower buds. The best time to make a cutting is when the plant has been well watered, by rain or artificial irrigation, especially in the early morning before the sun evaporates the water from the leaf surfaces.

Before making the cuttings prepare a flat with a mixture of coarse compost or sphagnum moss and builder's sand (don't use beach sand from the ocean, as the salt might kill the cuttings). Moisten the soil, poke holes 2 to 3 inches deep and 5 inches apart with your little finger, and take the flat to the garden. Select succulent stems that snap crisply when doubled over. Cut 6-inch pieces of rapidly growing shoots by making a diagonal slice through the stem with a razor blade. To encourage root formation, remove flower buds and leaves from the bottom 6 inches of the stem. Gently place the cutting into the hole and firmly press the soil around the base to assure good contact with the cutting. Then moisten the soil again.

Since the cuttings initially have no root systems, it is difficult for them to take up water. It is essential to keep the flats in the *shade* with the soil *moist*

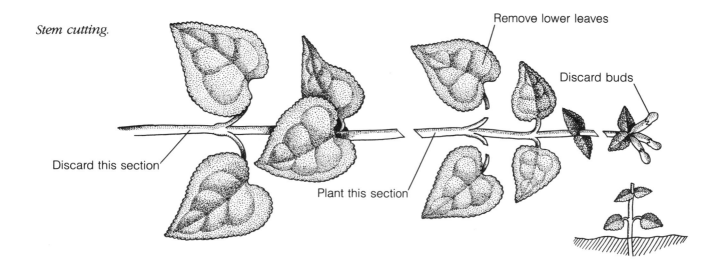

Stem cutting.

Remove lower leaves

Discard buds

Discard this section

Plant this section

but not wet. Soils that are too wet will prevent oxygen from getting to the developing roots and will also encourage rotting diseases. Protect the cuttings from the effects of drying winds, and mist the plants if the humidity is low. To attain ideal humidity control, put the entire flat in a large, *clear* polyethylene bag (available from janitorial supply companies), and tie off the opening. Another idea is to use a clear plastic garment bag to create a mini-greenhouse for starting cuttings. Allow the cuttings to remain in the flat until they go into dormancy at the end of the growing season, and then transplant them to holding beds or permanent locations.

Whether by collecting your own seeds or by dividing or cutting live plants, wildflower propagation can give you satisfactions beyond the considerable cost savings. Many perennials should be divided every several years, and they respond to this treatment by flowering more abundantly and adding even greater beauty to the garden. You can use the surplus divisions to enlarge your plantings, give them to other wildflower enthusiasts, or use them as material for container gardens. Perhaps one of the most important benefits of propagating plants yourself is the increased familiarity with wildflowers you gain in the process.

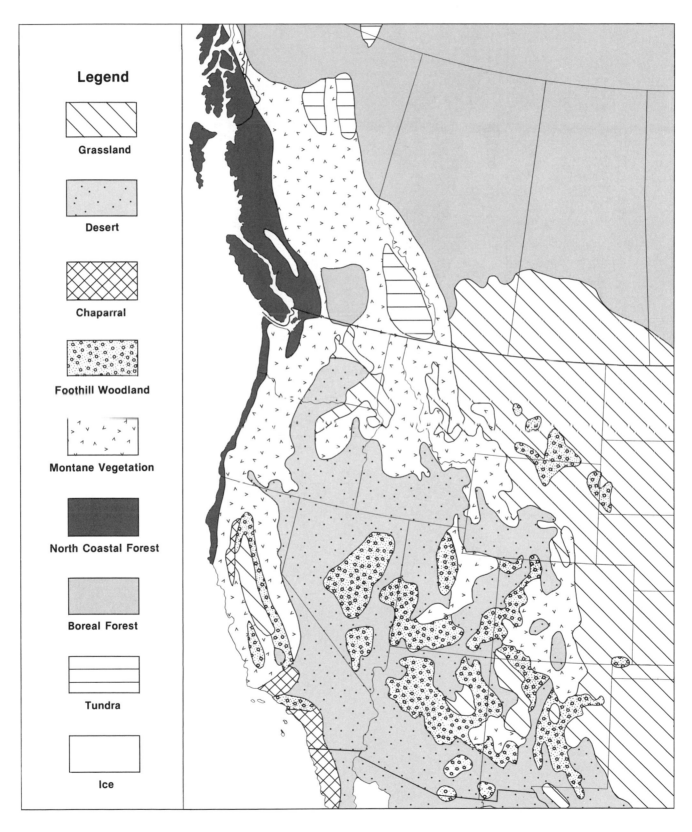

Legend

- Grassland
- Desert
- Chaparral
- Foothill Woodland
- Montane Vegetation
- North Coastal Forest
- Boreal Forest
- Tundra
- Ice

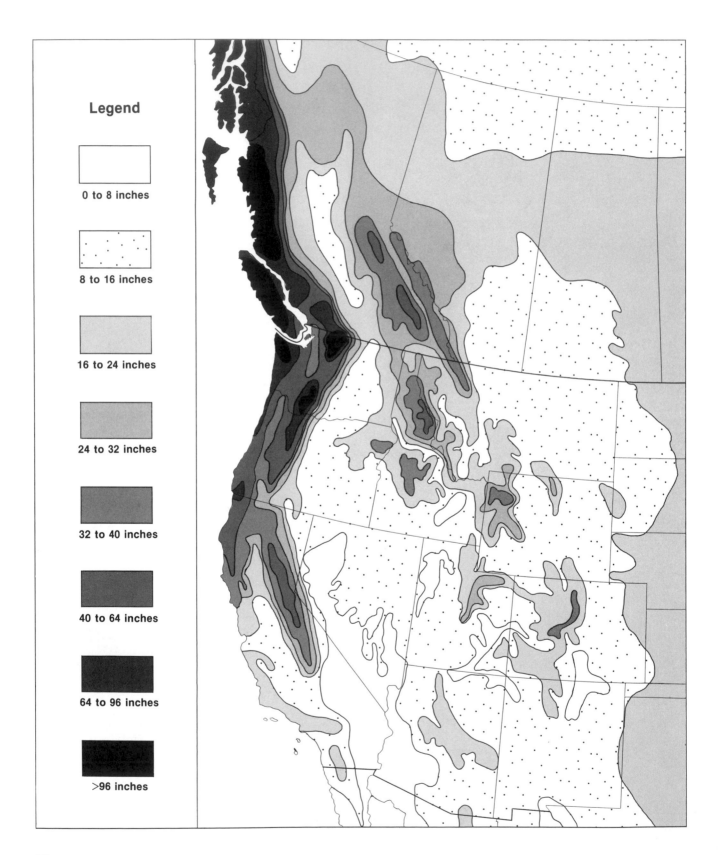

Legend

0 to 8 inches

8 to 16 inches

16 to 24 inches

24 to 32 inches

32 to 40 inches

40 to 64 inches

64 to 96 inches

>96 inches

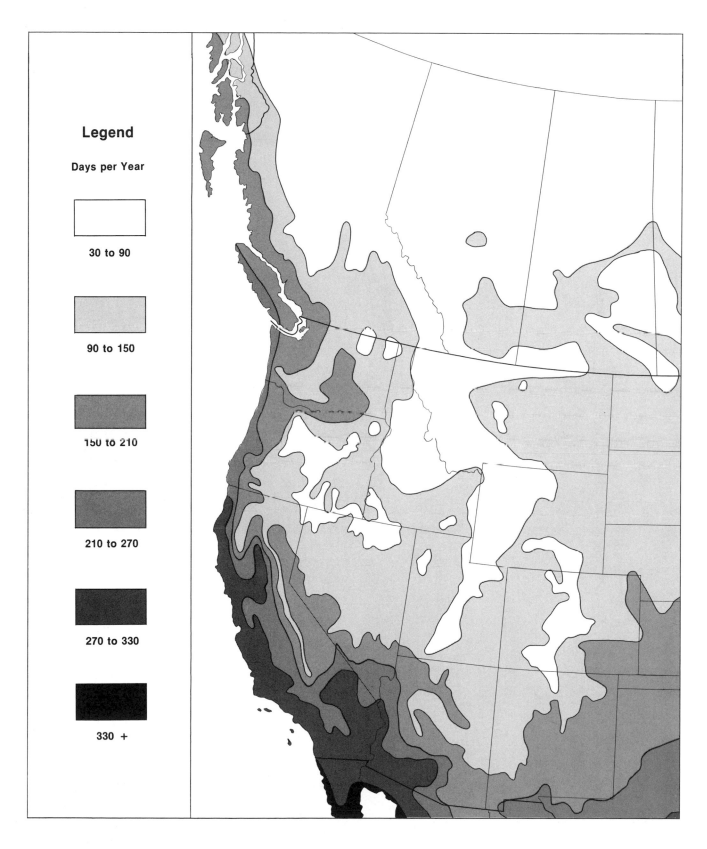

Legend

Days per Year

30 to 90

90 to 150

150 to 210

210 to 270

270 to 330

330 +

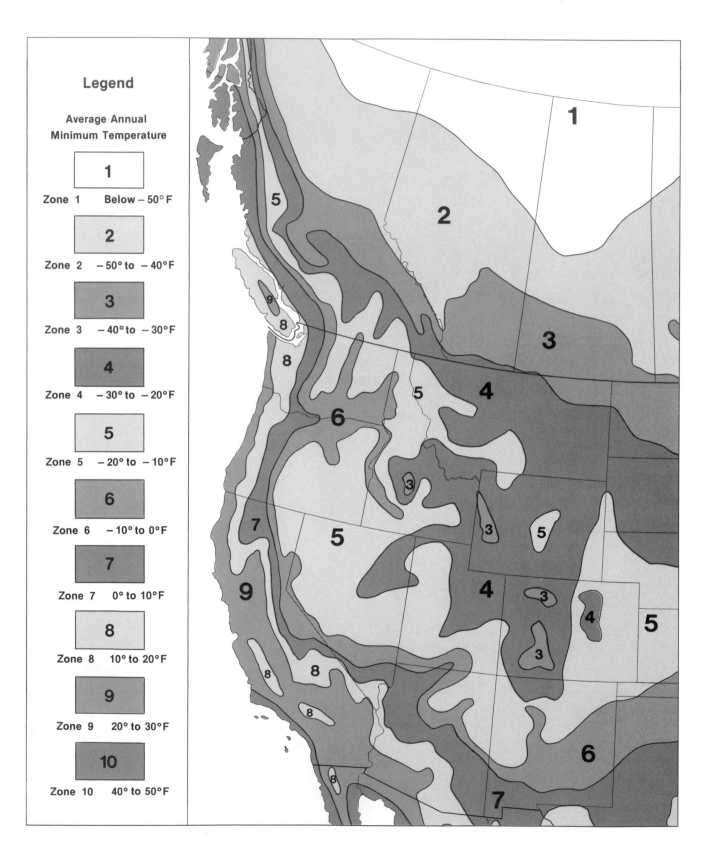

Legend

Average Annual Minimum Temperature

Zone 1   Below −50°F

Zone 2   −50° to −40°F

Zone 3   −40° to −30°F

Zone 4   −30° to −20°F

Zone 5   −20° to −10°F

Zone 6   −10° to 0°F

Zone 7   0° to 10°F

Zone 8   10° to 20°F

Zone 9   20° to 30°F

Zone 10   40° to 50°F

PART II

A Gallery of Northwestern Wildflowers

Farewell-to-spring provides the late spring garden with a patchwork of red, pink, and white. (See page 84.)

Clusters of soft pink **western bleeding heart** flowers hang over a carpet of fernlike leaves. (See page 86.)

Maroon spots accent the bright orange flowers of **leopard lily**, an ideal wildflower for beds and borders. (See page 88.)

The lowermost flowers of **Washington lupine** bloom first, and it may take nearly all summer for flowering to reach the top. (See page 90.)

Giant evening primrose is one of the largest and showiest of the biennial evening primroses. Its flowers open in the evening and wither by the next day. (See page 92.)

The lush leaves of **redwood sorrel** form a natural ground cover under conifers in the Pacific Northwest. Both pink and white flower color forms can be found. (See page 94.)

Checker bloom has long been a favorite for rock gardens because of its attractive hollyhock-like flowers, interesting leaf variations, and compact size. (See page 96.)

The clusters of creamy white **western Solomon's seal** flowers produce speckled, ruby red berries by late summer. (See page 98.)

Giant trillium is a magnificent addition to the woodland garden and comes in color forms ranging from white to pink to deep red. (See page 100.)

The tall spike of **western monkshood** bears many deep-blue, helmet-shaped flowers that are pollinated by bumblebees. (See page 104.)

There are separate male and female **pearly everlasting** plants, but either can be used to make excellent dried flower arrangements. (See page 106.)

The knobbed spurs of the **Colorado columbine** contain sweet nectar that is sought by hawkmoths and bumblebees. (See page 108.)

Four white bracts surround the tiny **bunchberry** flowers. Bright red berries are produced by late summer and persist into the fall. (See page 110.)

Fireweed is one of the first wildflowers to appear after logging or a forest fire. Its magenta flowers produce long pod fruits containing hundreds of small, tufted seeds. (See page 112.)

Photo by J.R. Haller

The spectacular pink flowers of **bitterroot** appear in the spring just as its tufts of narrow leaves start to wither. After flowering, the plant recedes into its underground roots until the leaves appear again in the fall. (See page 114.)

Yellow fawn lily is one of the first flowers to appear in the Rockies as the snow melts in the spring. (See page 116.)

The sprawling form, attractive foliage, bright flowers, and edible berries of **Oregon grape** make it a highly desirable ground cover for well-drained situations. (See page 118.)

The flowers of **mountain bluebells** are pink while in the bud, but rapidly turn sky blue as they open and expand. (See page 120.)

Dense clusters of blue-violet **Platte River penstemon** flowers are borne on the upper half of its stem. (See page 122.)

All of the royal blue flowers of **Rocky Mountain penstemon** usually grow to one side of the stem. (See page 124.)

The delicate, light blue flowers of **harebell** sway atop slender stems arising from tufts of grasslike foliage. (See page 128.)

74

Mountain dryas, a slow-growing alpine wildflower, flowers rapidly and then produces fruits that turn from silky green to fuzzy white. (See page 130.)

The tufted shape and dense clusters of bright yellow flowers have made the **sulfur-flowered eriogonum** a favorite of rock gardeners. (See page 132.)

Old-man-of-the-mountain flower heads usually face eastward toward the rising sun. The disc flowers change, with age, from light yellow to tan. (See page 134.)

Each of the many flowers clustered on the stem of **elephantheads** resembles the head of a miniature pink elephant. It grows best in cold, wet soils. (See page 136.)

Some of the flowers of **sky pilot** smell sweet and others smell skunky, attracting different pollinators. (See page 138.)

Rocky Mountain beeplant, a relative of the spider-flower, has numerous long stamens and produces large amounts of nectar that attracts bees. (See page 142.)

A perennial of the dry foothills of the Rockies, **blanketflower** was introduced into European gardens shortly after its discovery by the Lewis & Clark Expedition in 1806. (See page 144.)

Scarlet gilia is one of the most spectacular wildflowers of the West. Its flowers, found in both scarlet or pink color forms, are pollinated by hummingbirds and hawkmoths. (See page 146.)

The sky blue flowers of **blue flax** arch to one side of the tall, slender stems. It is an ideal wildflower for dry meadows. (See page 148.)

Tufted evening primrose flowers open at night and attract hawk-moths with their sweet fragrance. The flowers turn pink in the heat of the next day. (See page 150.)

Mexican hat flowers come in both yellow and red color forms. It grows well in both dry meadows and well-drained gardens. (See page 152.)

Open western foothills are often dotted with **mule's ears**, a wildflower with sunflowerlike blossoms and large, dark green leaves. (See page 154.)

Photo by J.R. Haller

PART III

Species of Wildflowers

The following pages give detailed information about 33 species of wildflowers. The plants are grouped by their natural habitat and appear in alphabetical order by botanical names. Wildflowers within the groups can grow together as companions, but many of the species can grow in more than one habitat. Each habitat group is introduced by general comments, a wildflower garden plan, and suggestions of additional species not in this edition of *The Wildflower Gardener's Guide* that make appropriate companions. Further information on these companions can be found in *A Garden of Wildflowers* or other books listed in Appendix D.

Each of the 33 wildflowers included in this book is listed by its most frequently used common name as well as by its Latin scientific name. Other common English, Spanish, and French names are also given. The individual wildflower description starts with general information about the species and its ecology. A discussion of culture and growth requirements follows, with specific directions for the plant's propagation. A few companions that grow under similar conditions are listed.

Each species is illustrated. A scale shows the approximate size of the plant, and a quick reference box shows plant family, flower color, flowering time, growth cycle (annual, biennial, or perennial), habitats where the species naturally occurs, and hardiness zones where the species can be grown. The map shows the wildflower's native distribution, but most species can be grown over a much wider area.

NORTH COASTAL FOREST SPECIES

The species presented in this section are adapted to survive in the ocean-moderated environments along the Pacific Slope and coast. Some of these species grow in sunny sites near the coast with well-drained soils, and others grow on damp soils in the shade of magnificent conifer forests. For the most part, the moderating effects of the Pacific Ocean make temperatures relatively unchallenging to gardeners. Both winters and summers are cool, often making the onset of spring a slow process. Winter minimum temperatures are highly variable from year to year, however, especially in areas protected from direct maritime influences, so the gardener should take precautions to mulch perennials even if the previous winter brought few frosts.

Soil drainage is a critical factor in the north coastal forest region. Some species need year-round moisture, but grow poorly in soils that are wet and boggy. Other species grow best on soils that are quite well drained. Wildflower gardeners need to pay attention to both species preferences and local conditions.

A great variety of native plants are available for use in north coastal forest areas. In addition to the species contained in this section, **wild ginger** (*Asarum caudatum*), with its broad, heart-shaped leaves and peculiar brown flowers, and **piggy-back-plant** or **youth-on-age** (*Tolmiea menziesii*), with its delicate, fuzzy, younger leaves appearing to perch on the older leaves, make attractive ground covers for the shady garden. **Western columbine** (*Aquilegia formosa*) has attractive, inch-long, pendant, red and yellow flowers; **Douglas's iris** (*Iris douglasiana*) comes in a range of colors from white to tan to light blue; **fairy bell** (*Disporum smithii*) has pink, bell-shaped flowers that produce large orange berries in the axils of its leaves: all are welcome additions to the rock garden or even beds and borders. If your garden is large, you may want to consider the stately 3-5-foot-high **sword fern** (*Polystichum munitum*) or the large but graceful **chain fern** (*Woodwardia fimbriata*).

Native woody plants should also be considered for north coastal forest landscapes: **rhododendron** (*Rhododendron macrophyllum*) is one of the most favored of native shrubs with its large, dark, evergreen leaves and clusters of pale purple

Pacific slope and coast garden.

A. Giant evening primrose
B. Western Solomon's seal
C. Western bleeding heart
D. Leopard lily
E. Giant trillium
F. Redwood sorrel
G. Washington lupine
H. Checker bloom
I. Farewell-to-spring

flowers; **thimbleberry** (*Rubus parviflorus*) has attractive, large, 5-lobed, pointed leaves and white flowers; and the **salal** (*Gaultheria shallon*) is a low shrub with evergreen leaves and clusters of white, pink-tinged, urn-shaped flowers. **Madrone** (*Arbutus menziesii*) is a medium-sized tree that also has clusters of urn-shaped flowers, but they are creamy white and produce orange berries. Its smooth flaky bark provides an interesting textural contrast to its broad evergreen leaves. It grows best in sites with moist soils. **California bay** (*Umbellaria californica*) makes a good companion tree with its aromatic, lance-shaped, evergreen leaves. In the warmer parts of northwestern California and southwestern Oregon, **tan oak** (*Lithocarpus densiflorus*) with its leathery, thick, gray-evergreen leaves is a superb small tree to plant on the edges of the garden. **Western flowering dogwood** (*Cornus nuttallii*) is a spectacular small tree suitable for more inland sites. It grows 30-60 feet high and has many clusters of small green flowers surrounded by 4 large, creamy, petallike bracts, filling the spring with splashes of white.

FAREWELL-TO-SPRING

Clarkia amoena
(Godetia amoena)

(Summer's darling, herald-of-summer, godetia, *adios primavera*)

Many of this plant's common names — farewell-to-spring, *adios primavera*, herald-of-summer, and summer's darling — refer to its flowering at the end of the spring and beginning of the summer. Native to coastal California and Oregon, this annual is named in honor of Captain William Clark, and not long after the Lewis and Clark expedition *Clarkia* was introduced by the Scottish botanist David Douglas into Europe as a garden flower. Much horticultural manipulation of this species has followed, and many varieties are now available through seed catalogs. Farewell-to-spring stands 1½–2½ feet tall and has linear, 1–3-inch-long leaves scattered along its stem. In the notches of several of the uppermost leaves are pink, cup-shaped, 2–4-inch flowers with 4 fan-shaped petals, blotched with dark red at their bases. White and lavender forms of this species also occur. Below the flowers are 4 reddish sepals, which often remain attached by their tips even after the flower bud has opened. In the center of the flower a 4-part white stigma tops the pistil, and 8 stamens rest against the petals. The flowers usually open during the day and close at night. The tapering, 1–2-inch-long capsular fruit with 4 grooves contains many tiny brownish seeds. Farewell-to-spring makes an attractive cut flower, which lasts for several days.

CULTURE: Farewell-to-spring can be grown in full sun to light shade. The soil should be moist but not wet until flowering starts, and then it can be quite dry. Warm, light, sandy loams are best, although heavier soils are tolerated if they are well drained. Do not apply additional fertilizer or the plants will become too tall and "leggy."

PROPAGATION: This hardy annual can be propagated only by seed, but it is easy and generally takes less than 90 days from seed to flowering plant. In coastal and hot desert regions seeds can be planted in the fall, but elsewhere they should be planted in the spring as soon as the soil starts to warm. Scratch the seeds into the soil surface in the desired location, and keep the soil moist until seeds germinate a week or two later. No chilling treatment is needed, but germination tends to be most rapid when the soil temperature is not excessively high. Thin seedlings to 6–9 inches apart.

COMPANIONS: Washington lupine, checker bloom, giant evening primrose, leopard lily.

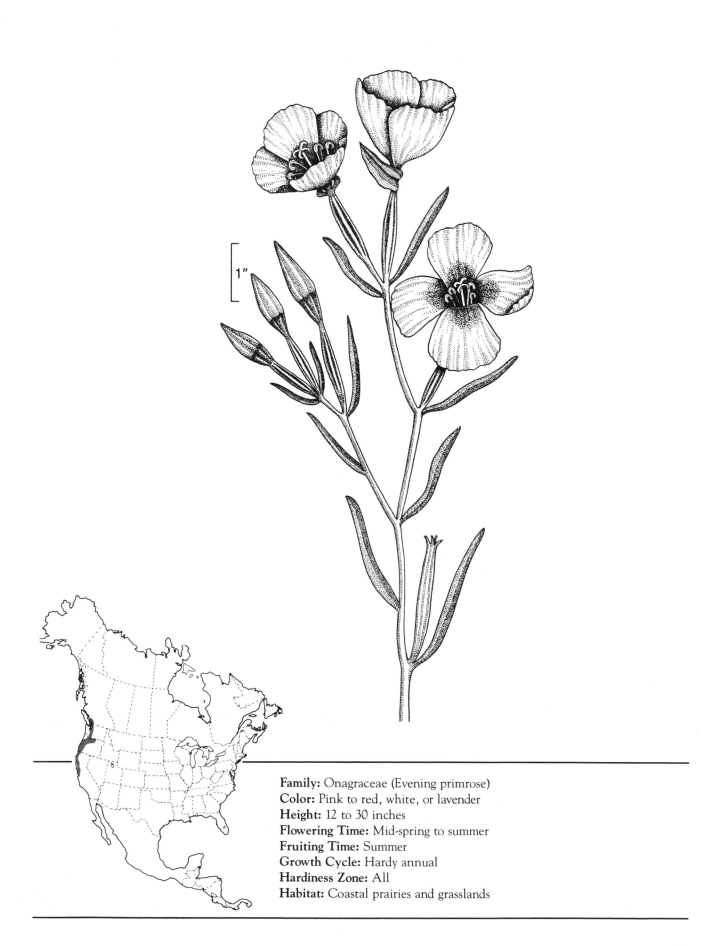

Family: Onagraceae (Evening primrose)
Color: Pink to red, white, or lavender
Height: 12 to 30 inches
Flowering Time: Mid-spring to summer
Fruiting Time: Summer
Growth Cycle: Hardy annual
Hardiness Zone: All
Habitat: Coastal prairies and grasslands

FAREWELL-TO-SPRING (*Clarkia amoena*)

WESTERN BLEEDING HEART *Dicentra formosa*

This wildflower is like a smaller version of the commonly grown bleeding heart (*Dicentra spectabilis*) from Japan, but it flowers from spring to late summer, even into early fall with sufficient moisture. Western bleeding heart has been popular in the gardening trade long enough for there to be several horticultural varieties, in addition to its natural subspecies, that are distinguished by differences in flower color and height of plant. Its attractive, bright green leaves with whitish undersurfaces appear in the early spring, remain lush during the summer, and then abruptly yellow and die in late summer. Its 9–20-inch-long, broadly triangular leaves are deeply dissected and fernlike. As with other members of the fumatory group in the poppy family, the leaves contain protopine and other alkaloid compounds that are toxins with narcotic effects. These deter most insects, although the yellow- or red-spotted black caterpillars of the clodius parnassian butterfly (*Parnassius clodius*) are unaffected, feeding almost exclusively upon this plant's leaves. Shortly after the leaves appear in the spring, 8–18-inch-high leafless scapes bearing clusters of 5 to 15 pendant flowers arise from the stout, tuberous, horizontal rhizome. To the human eye the flowers range in color from pink to magenta or, in some forms, yellow and white. The petals, however, contain pigments that strongly absorb ultraviolet light, so the flowers appear dark to bees, their main pollinator. The ¾-inch-long, heart-shaped flowers have a pair of small, purple, oval sepals and 4 petals arranged in 2 pairs. The outer pair forms the top of the heart and surrounds the inner pair, the tip of the heart, which encloses the 6 stamens and single pistil with its 2-horned stigma. The fruit is a ½–1-inch podlike capsule containing many small black seeds with a piece of white tissue called an *elaiosome*.

CULTURE: Western bleeding heart thrives in moist woodland soil with light shade or filtered sun. It is an excellent choice for the shady rock garden or for a ground cover under deciduous trees. The soil should be rich in organic matter, well drained, and moist but not wet. The roots will rot if the soil is wet.

PROPAGATION: It is easiest to propagate western bleeding heart by dividing the fleshy rhizomes and tubers during the autumn or early spring before leaves appear. Plant large tuber divisions about an inch deep and smaller tubers about ½ inch deep, and then mulch. This wildflower can also be propagated from seed. Collect fresh seeds in the summer, remove the elaiosomes, plant seeds outdoors ¼ inch deep, and mulch lightly. Seeds need moist, cold stratification for 3 months at 40°F if they have not been given a natural overwinter treatment outdoors. The seed is slow to germinate, so be patient. It will take several years for plants from seed to grow to flowering size.

COMPANIONS: Washington lupine, leopard lily, western Solomon's seal, giant trillium.

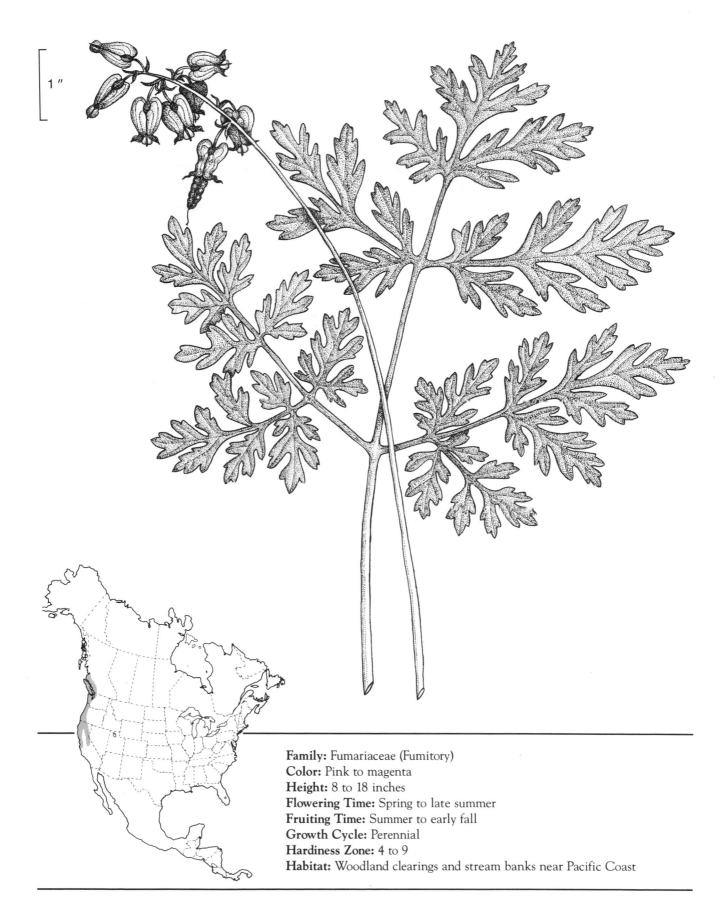

1 ″

Family: Fumariaceae (Fumitory)
Color: Pink to magenta
Height: 8 to 18 inches
Flowering Time: Spring to late summer
Fruiting Time: Summer to early fall
Growth Cycle: Perennial
Hardiness Zone: 4 to 9
Habitat: Woodland clearings and stream banks near Pacific Coast

WESTERN BLEEDING HEART *(Dicentra formosa)*

LEOPARD LILY

Lilium pardalinum

(Panther lily)

Bright orange flowers with dark spots appear in early summer around springs and streams in the mountains of northern California and southern Oregon, yet this perennial seems equally at home in formal beds and borders at lower elevations. Its 2-foot stems bear 3 to 4 whorls of smooth, linear, lance-shaped, pale green leaves that are 4–6 inches long and up to an inch wide, with additional leaves often scattered along the stem. The 2 to 5 nodding, 2–4-inch flowers arising from the top of the stem lack much in the way of fragrance, but compensate by their spectacular colors. The 3 petals and 3 identical petallike sepals are usually yellow at the base, with subtle gradations through orange and red to dark red toward the tip. Both the common name and the Latin name *pardalinum* refer to the scattered maroon leopard spots, most abundant near the petal bases. The petal tips curve back to touch the peduncle, or flower stalk, giving the elongated pistil with its rounded stigma and the 6 stamens a thrusting appearance. Each 2–3-inch-long filament connects to the middle of a large (½-inch) red anther. The fruit, an inch-long capsule, produces many flat, ¼-inch seeds. The 2–4-inch-long bulbs are branching and somewhat rhizome-like, covered with dense, white scales. With time, the many small bulblets formed by the main bulb enlarge and large colonies are produced. A number of natural varieties and horticultural cultivars of leopard lily have been refined over the years. These vary in flower color (variety *luteum* has yellow flowers), leaf width (variety *angustifolium* has narrow leaves), and plant height (variety *pallidifolium* grows 6-8 feet, and variety *giganteum* may top 8 feet and bear up to 30 flowers).

CULTURE: Leopard lily grows naturally in damp streamside situations. In the garden plant in deep, loose, well-drained, continually moist but not wet soil of slight acidity (pH 6-7). If the soil is clayey, add sand and copious amounts of organic matter. After flowering and fruiting the top of the plant withers; allow the leaves to turn completely yellow before cutting leaves and stems back. This hardy (zones 3-9) and robust perennial is the easiest of the Pacific Coast native lilies to grow and maintain, quite resistant to disease, and widely available.

PROPAGATION: Propagated from seed, leopard lily takes 4 to 5 years to flower; bulb divisions can cut this time in half. In the early spring, divide the ½-inch scales and entire bulblets from mature bulbs that have become overly crowded, and then replant them 18 inches apart, 4-6 inches deep. Since it takes several years for newly divided plants to flower, do not divide all your leopard lilies in a single year.

COMPANIONS: Western bleeding heart, Washington lupine, farewell-to-spring, giant evening primrose, checker bloom.

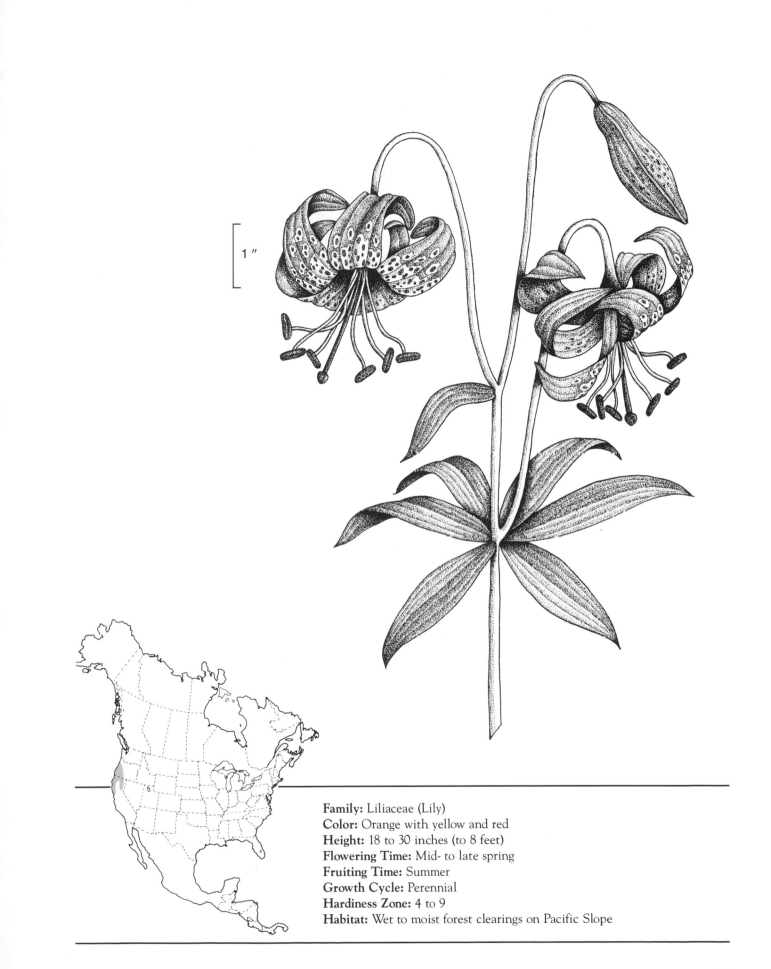

Family: Liliaceae (Lily)
Color: Orange with yellow and red
Height: 18 to 30 inches (to 8 feet)
Flowering Time: Mid- to late spring
Fruiting Time: Summer
Growth Cycle: Perennial
Hardiness Zone: 4 to 9
Habitat: Wet to moist forest clearings on Pacific Slope

LEOPARD LILY (*Lilium pardalinum*)

WASHINGTON LUPINE

Lupinus polyphyllus

(Blue-pod lupine, large-leaved lupine)

This native of northern California and the Pacific Northwest has become a world traveler. Introduced into European gardens in 1826, Washington lupine was quickly adopted as a desirable ornamental as well as a fodder crop, and now is widely naturalized there. George Russell of Yorkshire, England used this species as the parent stock in the creation of his famous Russell hybrid lupines. It naturally hybridizes with other lupine species in its native range. The new foliage of this perennial appears in early spring when the compound leaves with 10 to 17 lance-shaped leaflets emerge in a cluster from the soil. The palmately arranged leaflets then expand on a 6-inch-long petiole. The bright green leaves have a sparse undercoating of fine silvery hairs. Flowering begins in mid-spring and frequently lasts to mid-summer, starting at the bottom of the showy 6–24-inch spikes of blue and white flowers arranged in tiers of about 9 to 10 flowers each on the 1 ½–5-foot unbranched stems. Reddish, purple, and yellow flowers also appear. The bumblebee pollinators get no nectar reward for their work, but keep some pollen as they clamber up through the flower clusters. The wooly, 1–2-inch pod fruit, containing 5 to 9 mottled, 1/5-inch seeds, turns dark brown at maturity. The leaves contain alkaloid compounds, which deter insects ranging from grasshoppers to spruce budworms from eating the leaves. Some species of blue butterflies, however, are unaffected by these alkaloids, and even use them to signal where their caterpillars can obtain a good meal.

CULTURE: Washington lupine needs adequate moisture available throughout the year, but not saturated soils, because it is susceptible to powdery mildews. It grows best in slightly to moderately acidic soils (pH 5.0-7.0), but if your soils are rich in serpentine try growing the dwarf "Minarette" variety. Plant in full sun to partial shade, with good air circulation. It likes cool summers, so doesn't do well in Southern California. Lupine aphids may be a problem, but are preyed upon by fungi and the larvae of syrphid flies. Control aphids with insecticidal soap if natural agents are lacking. Do not use nitrogen fertilizers since they harm the bacteria *Rhizobium lupini*, which form small, light brown nodules in the roots and enable the plant to obtain nitrogen from air. If these bacteria are not present in your soil you may need to inoculate with rhizobia of the Nitragin Lupinus Special #3 type.

PROPAGATION: Easy to grow from seed even though germination may be slow. No seed treatment is necessary for fresh seeds, but dry seeds need scarification. Plant fresh seed ¼-½ inch deep in the desired locations. Or grow in flats and transplant seedlings when small, because established lupines don't move around well.

COMPANIONS: Leopard lily, giant evening primrose, western bleeding heart, checker bloom.

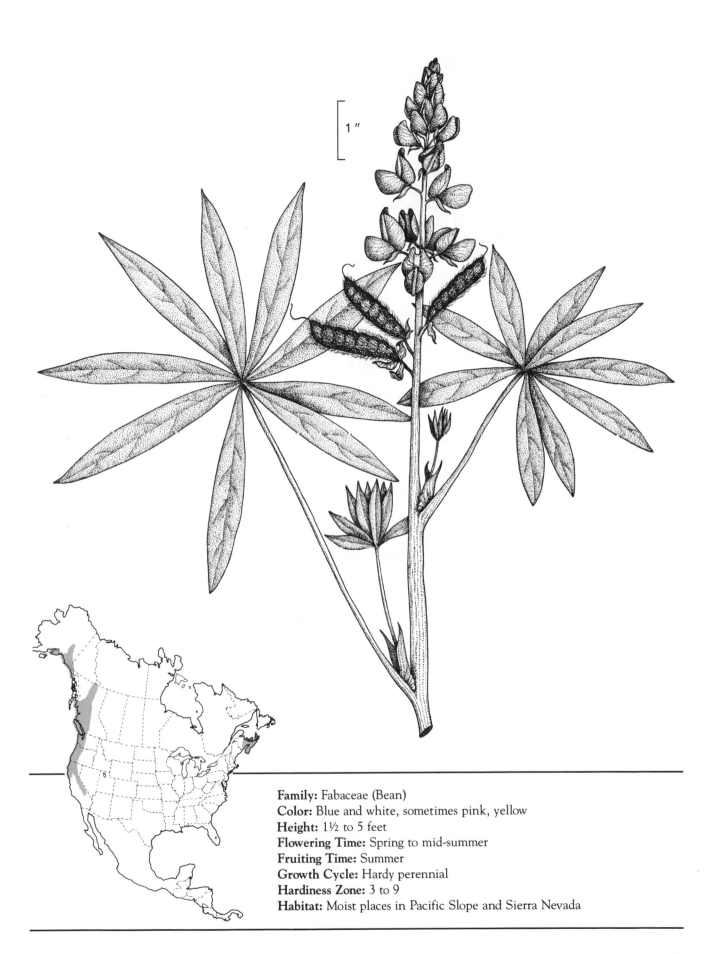

1 "

Family: Fabaceae (Bean)
Color: Blue and white, sometimes pink, yellow
Height: 1½ to 5 feet
Flowering Time: Spring to mid-summer
Fruiting Time: Summer
Growth Cycle: Hardy perennial
Hardiness Zone: 3 to 9
Habitat: Moist places in Pacific Slope and Sierra Nevada

WASHINGTON LUPINE (*Lupinus polyphyllus*)

GIANT EVENING PRIMROSE

Oenothera hookeri
(O. elata subsp. *hookeri)*

(Hooker's evening primrose, *coscatlacualtzin, hierba de Santiago*)

One of the largest and showiest of the evening primroses, this taxonomically diverse plant has several naturally occurring subspecies with varying heights and flower sizes. The giant evening primrose is usually 3-5 feet tall, although plants are reported to range from 1-9 feet in height. Regardless of the eventual height of the stem, this biennial spends its first year as a low rosette of leaves. The second year the stem bolts and numerous 5–10-inch-long leaves appear scattered along the reddish stem. The leaves, stems, and bases of the flower clusters are frequently covered with soft hairs. Clusters of bright yellow, saucer-shaped flowers are borne at the tops of the stems. Each of the 2½–3½-inch flowers has 4 broad petals which one can watch unfurl in late afternoon or at dusk. To the human eye the petals appear to be a uniform rich yellow, but to the bees that pollinate this species during the day and can see ultraviolet light, the flowers display yellow and purple petals. Hawkmoths also pollinate giant evening primrose, but at night. The evening blossoming of the flowers gives this plant its common name, although it is not related to the true primroses. The short-lived flowers wither in the noonday sun, turning orange with age. The fruit is a slender, woody, 1–2-inch-long capsule containing many tiny seeds. Twin seedlings can be produced by a single seed, but usually only one survives to maturity. Giant evening primrose is named in honor of the British botanist Sir William Jackson Hooker, a 19th-century director of the Royal Botanic Garden at Kew. Nighttime luminescence from rotting roots made Native Americans consider this a magical plant which, if rubbed on their moccasins and bodies, could help hunters find deer.

CULTURE:
Giant evening primrose should be planted in full sun and given ample room since it tends to become weedy. It is not fussy about soil acidity conditions, and while it grows best in moist soils, it also tolerates moderately dry soils. This biennial, an excellent plant for large damp meadows and streamside plantings, can be grown in hardiness zones 4-10.

PROPAGATION:
The easiest way to propagate giant evening primrose is from seed. Seed planted in the fall should be scratched into the surface of the soil where the plants are desired, and kept moist. No stratification of the seed is needed. Thin the seedlings to 12-18 inches apart or more. Seedlings will form a rosette the first season and flower the second season. As with other biennials, it is a good idea to plant the seeds 2 successive years to establish a continuously flowering population.

COMPANIONS:
Washington lupine, leopard lily, checker bloom.

Family: Onagraceae (Evening primrose)
Color: Yellow
Height: 3 to 5 feet
Flowering Time: Spring to fall
Fruiting Time: Summer to fall
Growth Cycle: Hardy biennial
Hardiness Zone: 4 to 10
Habitat: Moist soils from Pacific Coast to foothills

GIANT EVENING PRIMROSE (*Oenothera hookeri*)

REDWOOD SORREL

Oxalis oregana

(Oregon wood-sorrel, Oregon oxalis)

Oxalis is Greek for "sharp," referring to the sour taste of the foliage, but everything else about this species is soft. This stemless perennial, arising from creeping white rhizomes, forms dense carpets under redwoods and other conifers in the Pacific Northwest. The lush, 1–2-inch-wide shamrock-like leaves are made up of 3 heart-shaped leaflets with gray patches along the midribs and long hairs on their undersides. The leaves fold like a collapsing umbrella in the evening, and appear to droop into sleep overnight. In spring and summer, solitary flowers up to 1 inch wide, with 5 hairy sepals and 5 petals, arise from the scaly ends of the rootstocks. The pedicles (flower stems) and peduncles (leaf stems) are typically 1-3 inches long, succulent, and covered with rusty hairs. At the bases of the pedicles are two small, leafy bracts. There are both pink and white color forms of the flowers, and in both the petals have yellow splotches at their bases and lavender veins running to their tips. Inside the petals, 10 stamens encircle the 5-chambered superior ovary, topped by 5 styles. Redwood sorrel flowers tend to close at night and during cloudy weather. The fruit, a ⅓-inch egg-shaped capsule, discharges its 5 to 10 small seeds as the outside of the ripening ovary presses inward upon them.

CULTURE: Redwood sorrel needs the Pacific Northwest coastal climate — mild damp winters and cool moist summers of hardiness zones 8 and 9. It also grows best in acid soils (pH 4.5-6.5) rich in organic matter. This is a classic "shade plant" adapted to survival in shady environments, and it makes a superb ground cover in moist, shady locations where it won't be trampled. It can also be grown as a container plant for shady areas, keeping the soil moist but not wet. The container should be moved to a cooler location during the winter.

PROPAGATION: Propagate redwood sorrel from divisions of mature rhizomes made in the early spring and replanted to a depth of ½ inch. It can also be easily propagated from seed. The seeds require no special treatment; just plant them by scratching them into the soil surface. Keep the seedbed moist from the time they are planted until seedlings are well established.

COMPANIONS: Western Solomon's seal, giant trillium.

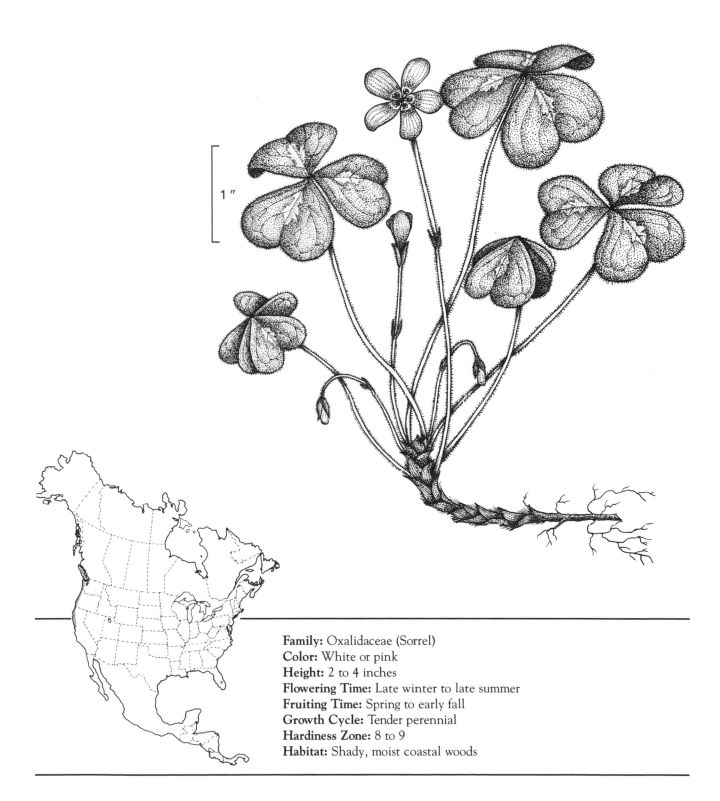

1″

Family: Oxalidaceae (Sorrel)
Color: White or pink
Height: 2 to 4 inches
Flowering Time: Late winter to late summer
Fruiting Time: Spring to early fall
Growth Cycle: Tender perennial
Hardiness Zone: 8 to 9
Habitat: Shady, moist coastal woods

REDWOOD SORREL (*Oxalis oregona*)

CHECKER BLOOM

Sidalcea malvaeflora

(Wild hollyhock, checker mallow)

Checker bloom produces miniature pink hollyhocks in the late winter and spring-time along the Pacific Coast and on the low elevations of inland California. This perennial has somewhat fleshy, slightly fuzzy, 1–2-inch-broad leaves with long stalks that emerge in a clump from the extensive, thick, woody root. The first leaves to appear are round and geraniumlike with pie-crust edges, but the later leaves, scattered along the semi-erect stems, are more deeply cut, like a bird's foot with 5 to 7 toes. The stems eventually reach 8-12 inches in height and bear up to a dozen or so inch-long flowers that open from the bottom toward the top over a 4-to-6-week period. The lavender to pink flowers, which open with the morning sun and twist closed at night, have raised white veins on their 5 petals and are joined at the base. The many stamens are fused together in 2 rings, forming a column in the center of the flower. Three to ten anthers, which turn rose-pink as they mature, are situated inside the stamen column, and the elongated style and stigmas grow outward through the anthers. As the fruit matures, the ovaries separate into flattened, 1/8-inch-wide seeds. Checker bloom has many varied sub-species distinguished by differences in growth form, leaf shape, degree of hairi-ness, and seed size. It is not uncommon to find the spiny, inch-long, brown and orange caterpillars of the West Coast lady butterfly (*Vanessa annabella*) feeding on the foliage of checker bloom.

CULTURE: Grow checker bloom in full sun to light shade on soils that are well drained but not excessively so. The soil should be kept moist during the winter and the spring flowering season, and then can be allowed to become drier. After the fruits have matured in the summer the dead shoots can be cut back to the ground. Checker bloom has long been a favorite of rock gardeners, even in England.

PROPAGATION: Checker bloom is most easily propagated from seed planted in the late fall. Ger-mination is enhanced if seeds are soaked in hot water overnight. Then plant the seeds about ¼ inch deep, and keep the soil moist, but not wet, until the seed-lings appear. In its native range, checker bloom self-seeds easily. Some plants from fall sowings produce flowers the first year and the remainder will bloom the fol-lowing spring. If given the proper conditions checker bloom will start to spread after several years. You can also propagate checker bloom by dividing the root crowns in the winter before the flowering stem starts to develop. Cut the root lengthwise into 2 to 3 pieces, each with several leaves and buds, and replant the cuttings 8-12 inches apart with the buds just at the ground level.

COMPANIONS: Farewell-to-spring, Washington lupine, leopard lily.

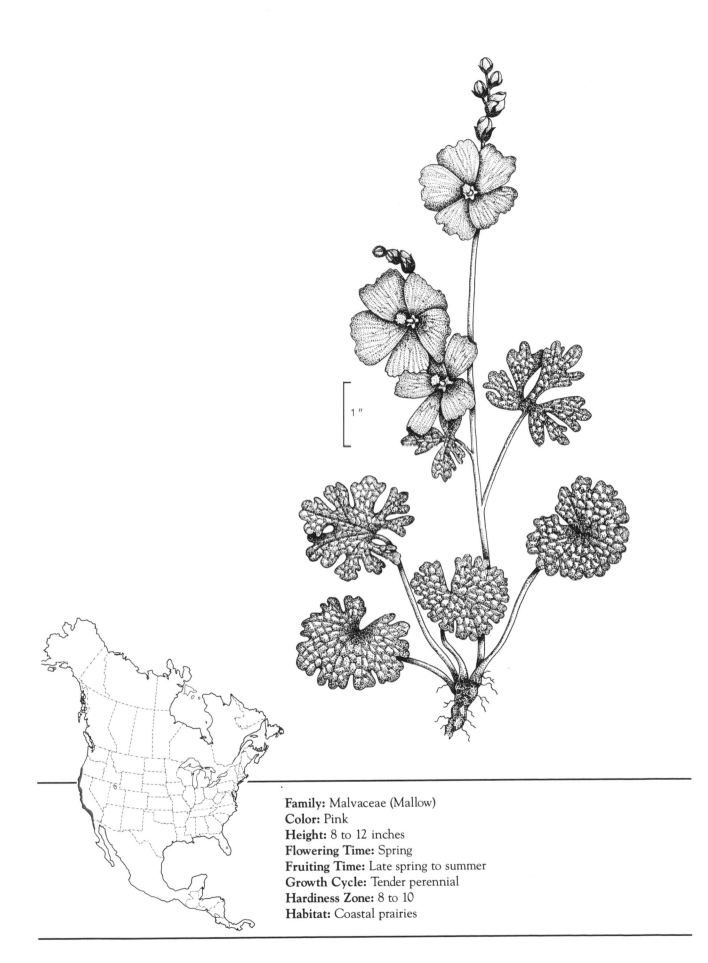

Family: Malvaceae (Mallow)
Color: Pink
Height: 8 to 12 inches
Flowering Time: Spring
Fruiting Time: Late spring to summer
Growth Cycle: Tender perennial
Hardiness Zone: 8 to 10
Habitat: Coastal prairies

1 "

CHECKER BLOOM (*Sidalcea malvaeflora*)

WESTERN SOLOMON'S SEAL   *Smilacina racemosa*

(False Solomon's seal, *smilacine à grappes*)

Western solomon's seal is the variety *amplexicaulis* of the species known in eastern North America as false Solomon's seal. It is distinguished from its eastern relatives by having longer plumelike flower clusters and shorter leaves. The ranges of the eastern and western varieties overlap in the Rockies. Like the true Solomon's seal (*Polygonum biflorum*), the western Solomon's seal has a knotted, thick rhizome, and 5 to 12 leaves in two rows along the stem. Clustered in 6–12-inch panicles at the ends of the arching, slightly zigzagged, 1–3-foot stems are the numerous, ¼-inch, creamy white flowers, each with 6 petallike parts. While many insects visit the flowers, some seeds appear to be produced without pollination. The fruits, 1/8-inch berries, contain 1 to 2 round seeds and turn from green to translucent ruby red dotted with purple as they ripen in late summer and early fall. You have to race the birds and small mammals to find the fruits, which are sweet smelling and edible despite their bitter aftertaste. Native Americans made a tea from the roots for treatment of internal pains.

CULTURE: The best situation for this hardy perennial is partial to full shade in soils that are moist and rich in humus. They will grow nicely in full sun or in drier situations, but tend to be somewhat stunted. In the shade seedlings are twice as likely to survive, and plants will be larger than in full sun. Western Solomon's seal does best in moderately acidic soils of pH 5-6.5.

PROPAGATION: Western Solomon's seal can be propagated by either rhizome division or seed. The plant naturally spreads by extension of its rhizomes and is easy to establish. Divide the rhizomes when the plant is dormant in the fall or early spring. Space the rhizome divisions, each with at least one bud, a foot apart, and place them horizontally at a depth of 1½ inches, with a thin layer of mulch to help retain moisture. The plants will generally flower the second year. For optimal germination, gather seeds as soon as the fruits ripen in the summer and do not let them dry out. Germination is greatly enhanced by cold, moist stratification (40°F for 3 to 4 months) and by darkness, since light inhibits the process. To guarantee darkness, leave an inch-thick mulch of deciduous leaves through the spring. Even under the best of conditions the seeds are slow to germinate, frequently taking 2 years, so be patient. If you plant them ¼ inch deep in flats that are left out over the winter, wait a second spring before discarding the soil. Have patience also as you wait for western Solomon's seal to flower when grown from seed. Seeds germinate in the spring, producing a 1–2-inch root and a minute shoot bearing only scale-like leaves. The next year a single leaf on a long petiole emerges from the bud. During the third year 2 leaves on a short shoot are produced. Flowers finally appear in the fifth year.

COMPANIONS: Redwood sorrel, giant trillium, western bleeding heart.

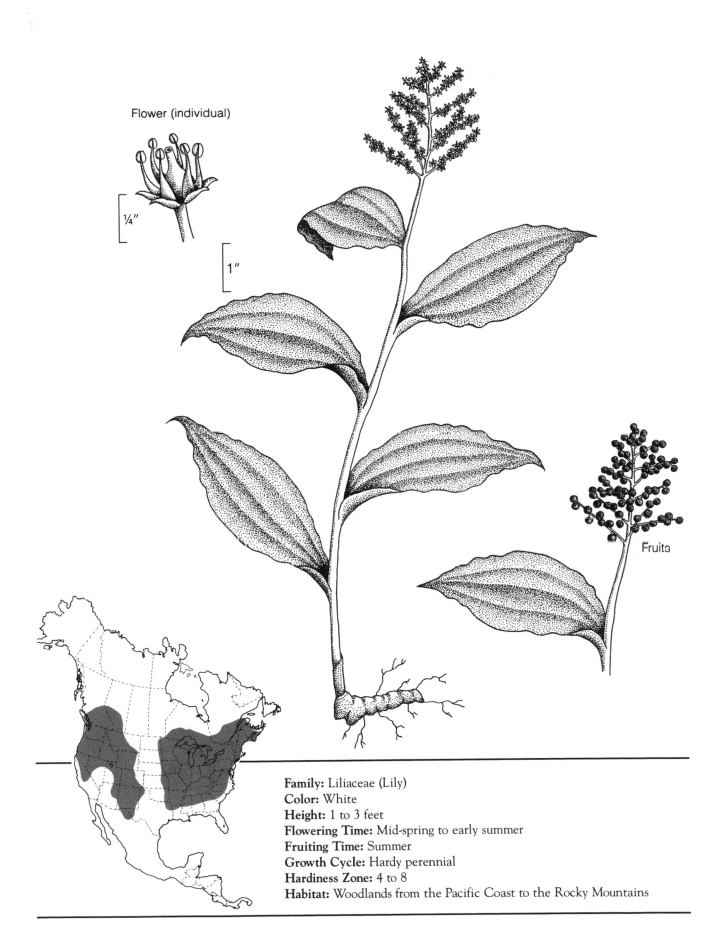

Flower (individual)

¼"

1"

Fruits

Family: Liliaceae (Lily)
Color: White
Height: 1 to 3 feet
Flowering Time: Mid-spring to early summer
Fruiting Time: Summer
Growth Cycle: Hardy perennial
Hardiness Zone: 4 to 8
Habitat: Woodlands from the Pacific Coast to the Rocky Mountains

WESTERN SOLOMON'S SEAL *(Smilacina racemosa)*

GIANT TRILLIUM

Trillium chloropetalum

This magnificent wildflower should never be molested in the wild. A perennial that grows slowly in rich, undisturbed northwestern forests, it should be considered for the garden only by those patient enough to propagate it from seed. The 3 mottled, 6-inch leaves are attached directly to the top of a 1½-foot stem. The shoot has a sheath at its base where it attaches to the deep, stout, bulbous, horizontal rootstock. The overlapping bases of the leaves surround the large, erect buds, which produce 4-inch flowers. Giant trillium can be found in a wide variety of color forms ranging from white to light green to pale yellow to pink tinged with purple to deep wine red and even brown. The lighter forms redden with age, possibly serving as a visual indicator to insects that pollination has occurred. Both the 2–4-inch upright petals and the 3 erect green 1–2-inch sepals surrounding them open as flowering progresses in late winter to late spring, depending upon location. The elongate stamens have short filaments supporting narrow, inch-long, yellow anthers, sometimes with red stripes. There are 2 sets of 3 stamens, the inner set covering the pistil as the flower opens. In the center of the flower is the 3-chambered superior ovary with 3 erect style branches, each ending in elaborately fluted stigmatic surfaces that become twisted about each other after pollination has occurred. As the ½-inch-long fruit ripens, the fleshy green oval berry becomes red then purple, and the sepals remain adhered to it. Inside the fruit are many small (1/10-inch) egg-shaped seeds. Native Americans used the very bitter roots to cure boils and as a strong medicine of last resort.

CULTURE: Giant trillium is a plant of moist soils in open woods of the Pacific Slope west of the Cascades. It prefers deep, well-drained soils rich in organic matter, slight to moderate acidity (pH 4.5-6.5), and ample moisture throughout the year. It grows in hardiness zones 6-9.

PROPAGATION: Giant trillium is not considered a "commercially viable species" since it takes as long as 5 years to produce plants of flowering size. Propagate it only from fresh seed, rather than purchasing plants, unless you can verify that the nursery has propagated plants and not dug wild plants. Given this warning, it should be added that giant trillium grows readily from seeds that are collected fresh and not allowed to dry out. Separate the dark red-purple flesh of the berry from the seeds, clean the seeds thoroughly, and plant them ¼ inch deep in a moist, humusy location. The seeds can also be planted in flats that are kept out during the winter, or from spring-planted seed that has been kept moist and stratified for at least 30 days at 40°F. First-year seedlings produce a single slender leaf. In the second year the leaf broadens, in the third year all 3 leaflets finally appear, but flowering typically doesn't start until the fifth year.

COMPANIONS: Western bleeding heart, redwood sorrel, western Solomon's seal.

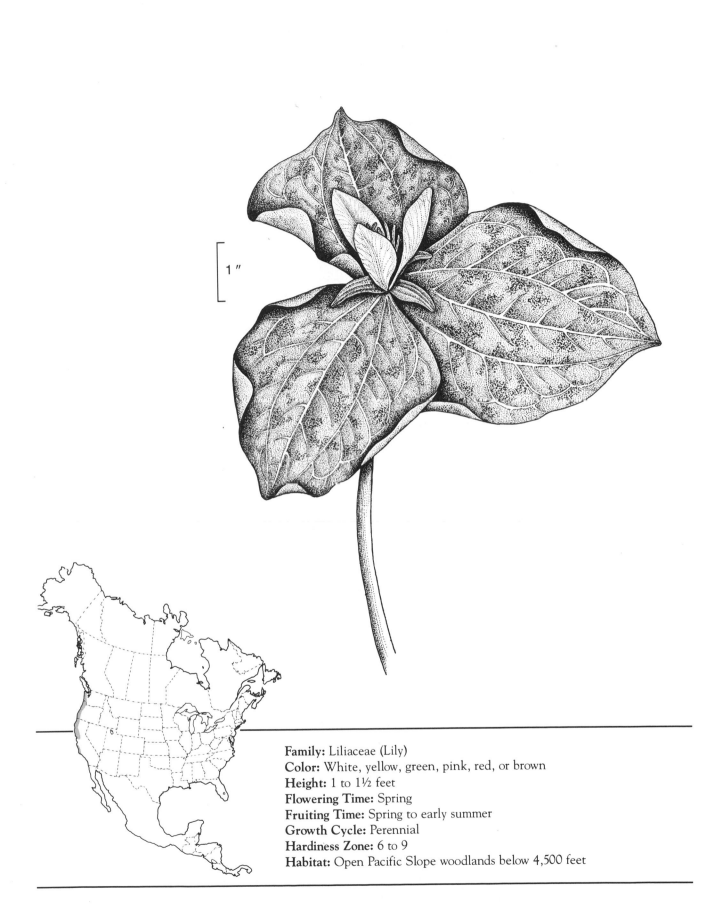

Family: Liliaceae (Lily)
Color: White, yellow, green, pink, red, or brown
Height: 1 to 1½ feet
Flowering Time: Spring
Fruiting Time: Spring to early summer
Growth Cycle: Perennial
Hardiness Zone: 6 to 9
Habitat: Open Pacific Slope woodlands below 4,500 feet

GIANT TRILLIUM (*Trillium chloropetalum*)

MONTANE FOREST SPECIES

The montane environments of the West, though different from one another, are variations on the theme of short growing seasons, warm summers followed by cold winters, and precipitation falling mostly as snow. As elevation increases from 7,000 to 10,000 feet, precipitation increases, air temperatures decrease, and growing seasons shorten. Conditions range from the bright sun of open meadows to the shade of aspen groves or conifer forests, providing many opportunities for montane gardening. The gardener should anticipate the warm, dry summer, taking advantage of the frequent, but brief, afternoon thunderstorms by situating gardens where rainwater collects.

Numerous native plants can make superb companions to the wildflowers included in this section. Some of the species included in foothill woodland and even north coastal forest sections of this book can be successfully grown in the montane garden if the spring microclimate is warm enough. Likewise, many of the alpine wildflowers can be successfully grown at lower elevations if protected from heat and drying winds.

Wildflowers to consider for dry sites include: Douglas's wallflower (*Erysimum capitatum*), a yellow-flowered biennial or tender perennial that can be grown in hardiness zones 6 and warmer; beargrass (*Xerophyllum tenax*), a handsome, white-flowered, 2–5-foot plant of the Cascades and Rockies; and wild bergamot (*Monarda fistulosa*), a member of the mint family with whorls of lavender flowers. Kinnikinnik or bearberry (*Arctostaphylos uva-ursi*) forms an evergreen mat bearing pink or white urn-shaped flowers that produce red, fleshy berries and is an ideal ground cover for dry sunny locations.

If your garden is on the cool and wet side, twinflower (*Linnea borealis*) forms a spreading mat with pairs of delicate pink funnel-shaped flowers arising from the evergreen foliage. Cardinal flower (*Lobelia cardinalis*) is a tall perennial that thrives in wet soils and has spikes of scarlet flowers resembling cranes in flight.

Montane garden.

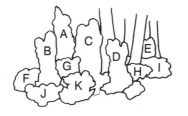

A. Fireweed
B. Rocky Mountain penstemon
C. Western monkshood
D. Platte River penstemon
E. Mountain bluebells
F. Pearly everlasting
G. Colorado columbine
H. Bunchberry
I. Oregon grape
J. Bitterroot
K. Yellow fawn lily

Native vines, shrubs, and trees are also appropriate additions to the montane garden. Fuzzy, feathery clusters of fruits and blue, petalless flowers make rock clematis (*Clematis columbiana*) an attractive climbing woody vine for sunny areas. Golden currant (*Ribes aureum*), an erect, spicy shrub with bright yellow spring flowers, and manzanita (*Arctostaphylos manzanita*), a small tree with twisted reddish bark and clusters of white flowers producing red berries, are two species worthy of consideration for well-drained gardens. Although ponderosa pine (*Pinus ponderosa*) usually grows at lower elevations than the more open and spreading white-barked pine (*P. albicaulis*), they both can be grown over a rather broad elevation belt as long as the site is not excessively hot in the summer.

WESTERN MONKSHOOD

Aconitum columbianum

(Columbia monkshood, monkshood, aconite)

A perennial with many regional variants that have long befuddled taxonomists, western monkshood usually has dark blue-purple flowers, but has white flowers in the Blue Mountains of Washington and Oregon. Near the smooth base of the 1½–6-foot stem the deeply clefted, 2–7-inch-wide leaves have 5 lobes and long petioles, but near the fuzzy top of the stem they have only 3 lobes and are attached directly to the stem. In early summer an 8–24-inch spike emerges with several dozen 1½-inch helmet- or hood-shaped flowers, inspiring this wildflower's common name. The flowers have 5 petallike sepals: 2 lateral wings surrounding the many stamens and 3 pistils; a pair of small, pointed basal sepals; and a peaked ¾–1-inch hood concealing the 2 small true petals and the elaborate, elongated, claw-shaped nectaries. Flowering starts at the bottom of the spike and progresses upward. When the flower opens it is in the male phase, its anthers releasing pollen. Several days later, the stamens have withered and the tips of the styles split open to reveal the stigmas, ready to receive pollen. When flowers are in this female phase, they start to produce abundant amounts of nectar. Although hawkmoths and humming-birds drink the nectar, western monkshood is pollinated *exclusively* by bumble-bees. The bees start at the bottom with the lowermost flower, brush past the stigmas, climb into the hood, and follow the nectary grooves until their tongues reach the sweet reward. They then work up the spike to the newly opened nec-tarless flowers to pick up a new load of pollen. This pattern encourages cross-pollination, although pollination can occur between flowers on the same stem. The ½–¾-inch follicle fruits contain many small, flattened seeds. The root sys-tems of western monkshood have inch-long torpedo-shaped tubers, and each year produce new offset tubers that overwinter. The roots and leaves produce varying amounts of several toxic diterpine alkaloid compounds, such as talatizamine and camaconine, that protect the plant from being eaten.

CULTURE: Grow western monkshood in locations with full sun to partial shade. It is not choosy about soil pH, prefers soils that are moist, but not saturated, and can be culti-vated in hardiness zones 4–9. Western monkshood is generally used as a border plant because of its height.

PROPAGATION: No seed treatment is necessary, but several months of moist stratification at 40°F may enhance germination. Plant fresh seeds ¼ inch deep in the desired location as soon as capsules open. New offset tubers can be divided in the spring, and replanted at the same depth. If your plant produces bulbils in the notches of the leaves halfway up the stem, collect them when they are plump, before they fall to the ground. Plant them ¼ inch deep in moist but not wet soil.

COMPANIONS: Fireweed, Colorado columbine, mountain bluebells, leopard lily.

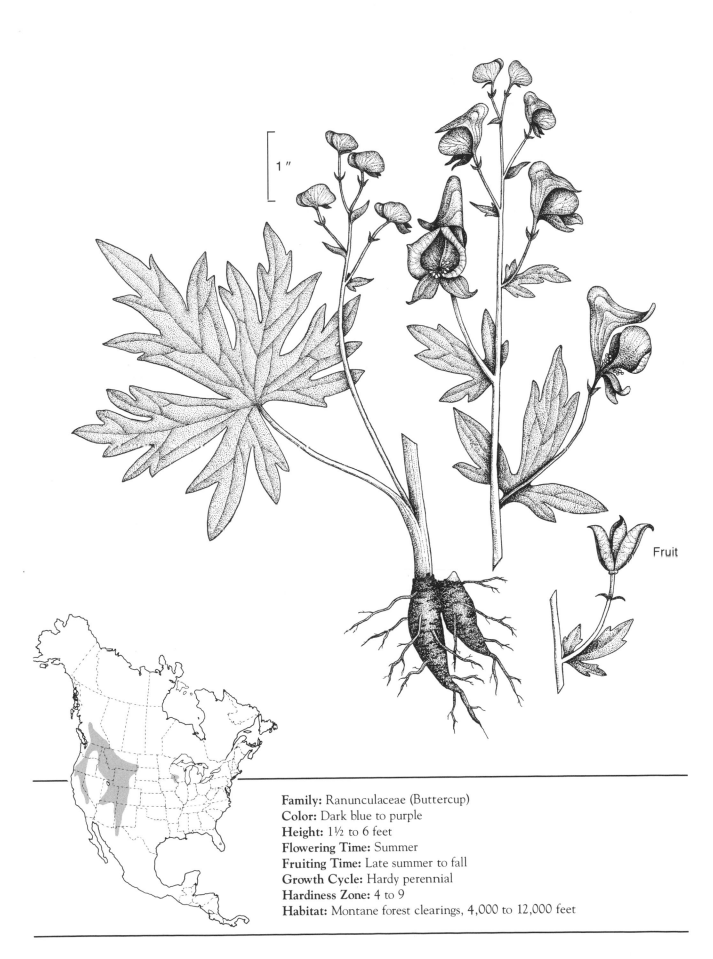

1″

Fruit

Family: Ranunculaceae (Buttercup)
Color: Dark blue to purple
Height: 1½ to 6 feet
Flowering Time: Summer
Fruiting Time: Late summer to fall
Growth Cycle: Hardy perennial
Hardiness Zone: 4 to 9
Habitat: Montane forest clearings, 4,000 to 12,000 feet

WESTERN MONKSHOOD (*Aconitum columbianum*)

PEARLY EVERLASTING *Anaphalis margaritacea*

(Silver-leaf, life everlasting, *immortelle*)

Found from coast to coast in North America (as well as in eastern Asia), this wild-flower fascinated early European explorers, who sent the plant back to the Old World in the 16th century for both its everlasting and its alleged insecticidal qualities. Pearly everlasting, an early colonizer of landslides and other disturbed sites, was one of the first plants to return to Mt. St. Helens after the May, 1980 eruption, and was well established within 5 years. The edges of its narrow, 1–4-inch, clasping, 1-to-3-nerved leaves sometimes curl under toward their wooly undersides. The upper surface of the leaf can be covered with silvery hairs, making it look light gray, but these often fall off and the leaf becomes green with age. The spatula-shaped leaves at the base and the scalelike ones low on the stem usually wither before the 8–24-inch-high stems start bearing clusters of numerous, small, rounded, ¼–½-inch flower heads in late summer through early fall. The Latin name *margaritacea* means "pearly," describing the white scales that encase the yellow-brown florets. Pearly everlasting are dioecious, that is, they have separate male and female plants, each bearing flowers. On the male flowers are clusters of florets, each with 5 small anthers, except for the sterile florets in the center. The female flower heads look quite similar except that the florets have two stigmas and no anthers. The seedlike, cylindrical, light brown fruits are topped by a plume of silky hairs and covered with very short hairs, aiding the wind dispersal of the fruits. The underground runners of this perennial send up new shoots each spring, forming colonies over time. Both the silvery hairs covering the plant and the large amount of tannin in the leaves protect the plant from sucking insects. Nevertheless, the American painted lady butterfly (*Vanessa virginiensis*) rears its 1¼-inch, yellow, black, red, white, and black caterpillars on the leaves of pearly everlasting, and its pupae build nests using the plant's silvery hairs. Native Americans used pearly everlasting to cure diarrhea and as an astringent for hemorrhoids. It was also smoked as a cure for coughs and as a substitute for tobacco.

CULTURE: Pearly everlasting grows well in dry, gravelly, sandy, well-drained soil, but benefits from moisture. It doesn't need extra fertilizer, but will grow to a larger size if extra nutrients are added. It is excellent in rock gardens or meadows in the full sun or light shade. For everlasting cut flowers, harvest stems in late summer before flowers are fully mature, remove some of the lower leaves from the stem, and hang bunches upside down in a cool, well-ventilated place until fully dry.

PROPAGATION: No seed treatment is necessary. In the fall, sow fresh seeds 1/8 inch deep in desired locations or start in flats and transplant 18 inches apart in the spring when seedlings are sturdy. Make rhizome divisions in the early spring, planting 18 inches apart and ½ inch deep.

COMPANIONS: Fireweed, blanketflower, harebell, sulfur-flowered eriogonum, many others.

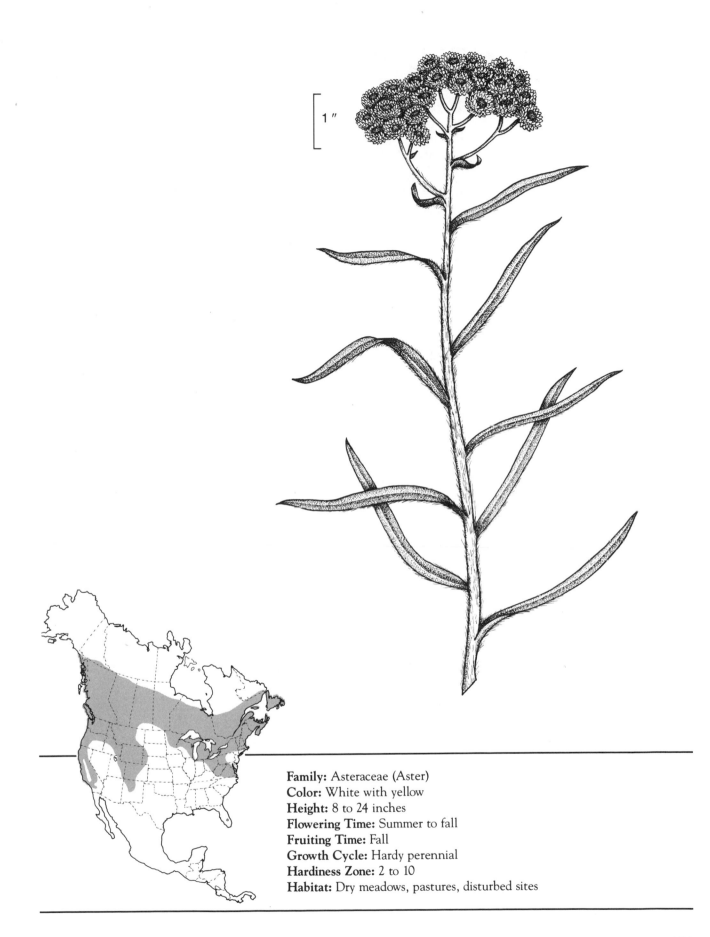

1 "

Family: Asteraceae (Aster)
Color: White with yellow
Height: 8 to 24 inches
Flowering Time: Summer to fall
Fruiting Time: Fall
Growth Cycle: Hardy perennial
Hardiness Zone: 2 to 10
Habitat: Dry meadows, pastures, disturbed sites

PEARLY EVERLASTING (*Anaphalis margaritacea*)

COLORADO COLUMBINE

(Rocky Mountain columbine)

The state flower of Colorado, this is a plant of moist aspen and pine groves. The smooth, divided, 1–3-foot-tall stems support the 3-part compound leaves with the rounded, indented leaflets typical of columbines. The wild columbine's flowers are more elegant than any garden-variety columbine. Nodding while in bud, the 2–3-inch, mildly fragrant flowers point slightly upward as they blossom. The most common variety of Colorado columbine has sky blue sepals and white petals, while other varieties are all white or all light blue. The 5 blue, fused, hooded, petallike sepals have knobbed, 2-inch spurs containing nectaries. Inside the sepals are 5 white petals, each with two rounded lobes. The petals surround the cluster of bright yellow stamens whose anthers give off pollen for the first 4 to 5 days that the flower is open. The stamens wither just before the pistils in the center of the flower become receptive to pollen for 3 to 4 days. The erect flowers are pollinated primarily by the white-lined sphinx moth (*Hyles lineata*), hawkmoths that drink nectar, and bumblebees that eat both pollen and nectar. Some bumblebees take a shortcut: they snip off the knob at the end of the spur and consume the nectar without pollinating the flower. Broad-tailed hummingbirds also frequently drink the nectar without pollinating the flower. Self-pollination is possible, but seed production is significantly higher where pollinators are active. The fruit is 5 connected pods containing small round seeds. Some of the most attractive long-spurred hybrid cultivars have been derived from this genetic stock.

CULTURE:
Although a hardy perennial of the Rockies, this columbine can be easily grown in hardiness zones 2-7. Plant in full sun to partial shade in locations receiving at least several hours of sun each day. The soil, which may range from rocky to sandy to loamy, should be moist but not overly wet or dry during the growing season. Colorado columbine does best in neutral soils (pH 6-8) with ample organic matter. Before planting, work compost 6 inches into the soil — but don't add so much that you make the soil slow to drain. A good cut flower.

PROPAGATION:
Propagation of Colorado columbine is best from fresh seed. Since germination is stimulated by light, scratch seeds lightly into the soil in a sunny location in permanent locations, nursery beds, or flats. Stratification is not necessary, but chilling (40°F) in moist sand for 2 months will accelerate germination, which may take a month in the spring. Keep moist until seedlings become established. Some plants from seed may flower the first year; most will the second year. Colorado columbine may die out after several years, so treat it as a biennial and plant seeds for two consecutive years. Once established, Colorado columbine will self-seed.

COMPANIONS:
Western monkshood, fireweed, Rocky Mountain penstemon, mountain bluebells, Washington lupine.

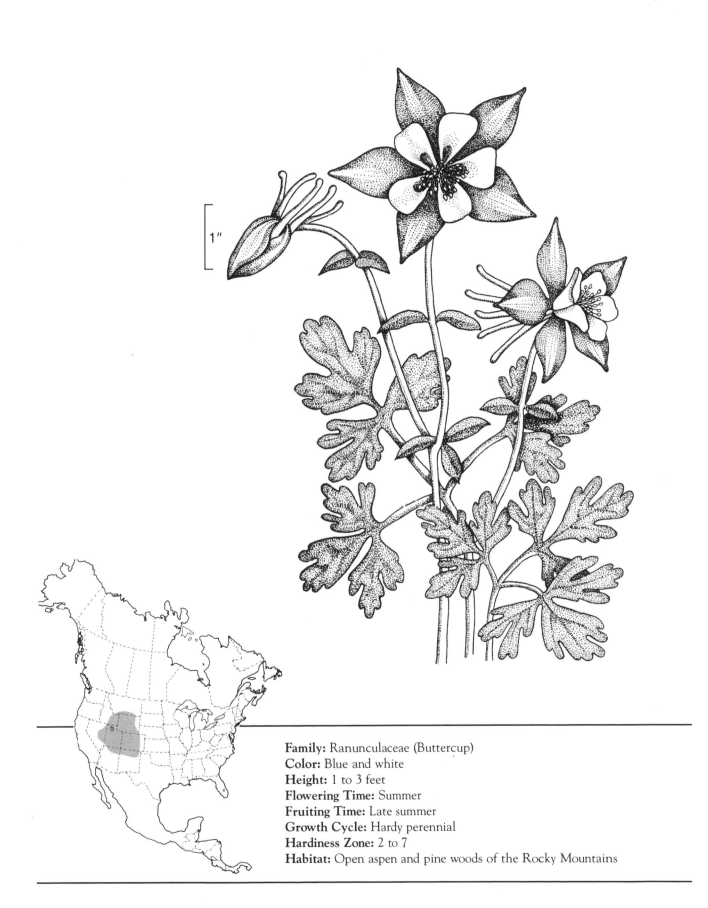

1"

Family: Ranunculaceae (Buttercup)
Color: Blue and white
Height: 1 to 3 feet
Flowering Time: Summer
Fruiting Time: Late summer
Growth Cycle: Hardy perennial
Hardiness Zone: 2 to 7
Habitat: Open aspen and pine woods of the Rocky Mountains

COLORADO COLUMBINE (*Aquilegia caerulea*)

BUNCHBERRY

Cornus canadensis

(Dwarf cornell, *cornouiller du Canada*)

This relative of the flowering dogwood tree attains a height of only 4-8 inches. Bunchberry spreads by means of slender, forking, woody rhizomes that creep along just under the ground litter, giving rise to attractive colonies and forming dense carpets with time. In the Rockies and in areas with cool autumn nights, the thick, lustrous leaves of bunchberry may turn from green to purple and even red before they fall. Whorls of 3 to 9 but usually 4 distinctively veined 1–3-inch leaves are overtopped by a cluster of small, greenish white flowers. What appear to be 4 creamy white petals are actually bracts, which fall away as the fruits develop. Bunchberry absolutely depends on the bumblebees, solitary bees, and beeflies that pollinate its flowers, and in years with bad weather or when pesticides have been sprayed for forest insect control, fruit production can completely fail. Normally, only about 10 percent of the flowers produce fruit. The bright red, berrylike, ¼-inch fruits, each with a 2-seeded light brown stone, cluster into spectacular bunches. The fruits, sometimes persisting into winter, are edible but relished only by birds, especially those in migration.

CULTURE: Bunchberry grows best in cool, damp, even wet locations in regions that do not have excessively hot summers. It is an ideal ground cover where there is partial shade and the soils are acid (pH 4–5), with ample conifer mulch and organic matter. In the sun the plant will do well, but its leaves tend to be much smaller, thicker, and not as deep green. Bunchberry roots are often infected with beneficial fungi known as *endomycorrhizae* which enable bunchberry to take up nutrients from the soil more efficiently. Therefore, do not use fungicides anywhere in the vicinity of this plant.

PROPAGATION: Bunchberry may be propagated by seed or by rhizome division. Harvest mature fruit in the fall, remove the stones from the pulp, and plant them ½ inch deep in a mixture of peat moss and sand. Keep the soil moist. Seeds require cold, moist stratification (40°F for 120 days) in order to germinate, and if planted in flats, they should be left outdoors for the winter. Germination of some of the seeds will occur 1 to 3 months into the spring, and the seedlings can be transplanted to permanent locations in the fall. You can add new seeds to the flats at this time and leave them out a second winter because many seeds planted the first year may not have germinated. Flowering usually occurs in the third year. Divide the rhizomes in the early spring or late fall. Cut 6-inch segments of the rhizome, each with at least one bud. Set the divisions ½ inch deep, mulch with conifer needles, and keep moist.

COMPANIONS: Yellow fawn lily, mountain bluebells, sky pilot.

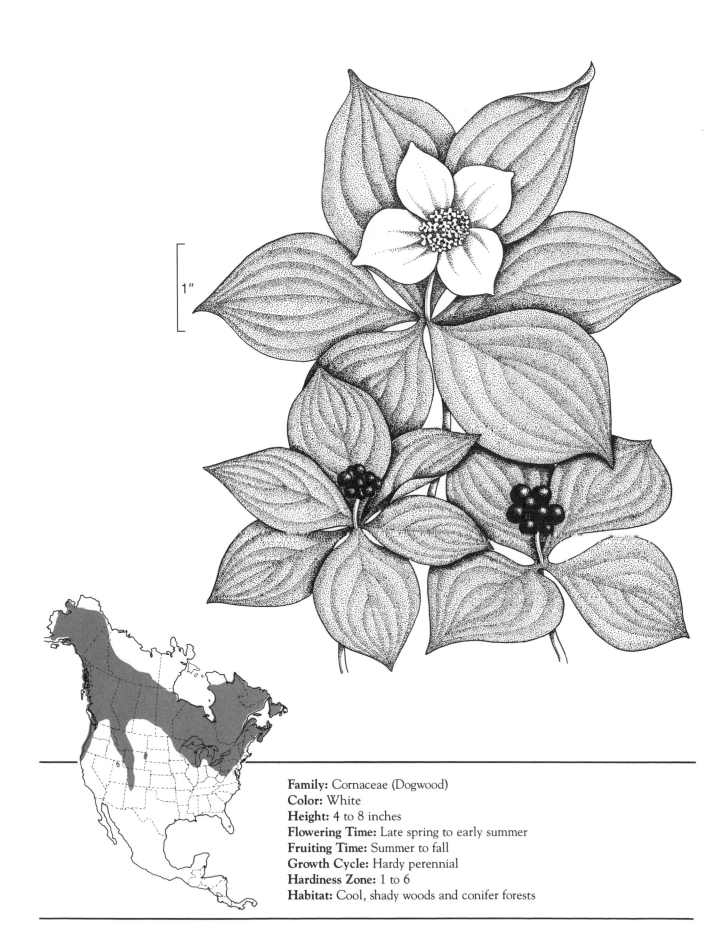

Family: Cornaceae (Dogwood)
Color: White
Height: 4 to 8 inches
Flowering Time: Late spring to early summer
Fruiting Time: Summer to fall
Growth Cycle: Hardy perennial
Hardiness Zone: 1 to 6
Habitat: Cool, shady woods and conifer forests

BUNCHBERRY (*Cornus canadensis*)

FIREWEED

Epilobium angustifolium

(Great willow herb, rosebay, blooming Sally, *epilobe à feuilles etroites*)

Although sometimes considered a plant of the Rockies and the Northwest, fireweed is a truly cosmopolitan wildflower found along the Pacific coast from Mexico to the Arctic, and around the world. Though named because it appears quickly after forest fires, this summer-flowering perennial soon establishes itself following any disturbance to the landscape — in bombed-out London during World War II and after the eruptions of Washington's Mt. St. Helens in 1980 and Alaska's Mt. Katmai in 1912. Reddish shoots emerge from the somewhat woody root crown and spreading rootstocks in the spring and remain red as the 2–7-foot stems produce narrow 2–5-inch lance-shaped leaves with short petioles. The Latin name *angustifolium* means "narrow leaf," and the common name "willow-herb" refers to the willowlike leaves. Near the edges of the leaves, with their pale green lower surfaces, are distinctive veins joined in loops. Up to 100 inch-wide flowers, their 4 sepals and 4 magenta to pink or even yellow petals forming a cross, are arranged in a foot-long spirelike raceme. Flowering starts at the bottom and proceeds toward the top, with only about 10 flowers open at a time. *Epilobium* is Latin for "flower upon the pod," as the inferior ovary is encased in a tubular, pubescent calyx with 4 lavender-tinged sepals. For several days after a new flower opens, its 8 anthers shed their sticky pollen. When the stamens wither, the style rises up and a cross-shaped stigma opens, then curling while exposed over the following several days. Fireweed's thin 2–3-inch pod fruits curl open when mature to release a cargo of 300 to 500 minute, tufted seeds. These float easily on the breeze, many rising 300 feet and traveling hundreds of miles. Even though the leaves are rich in tannin compounds, which help the plant resist being eaten by insects, they are enjoyed by many mammals. The roots and leaves were used by Native Americans and early European explorers for food and to cure stomach disorders; recently researchers have "discovered" anti-inflammatory compounds in extracts of fireweed.

CULTURE: Establish fireweed on bare mineral soil where it is sunny for at least part of the day. In the sun it can live for 20 years or more, but it dies out in shade. Tolerant of soils with pH 3.5–8.5, it grows best at pH 6–7. Fertilizing will produce larger plants. It prefers moist soils, but tolerates fairly dry soils. It can be aggressive, spreading rapidly by its underground rhizomes, and so is useful for erosion control.

PROPAGATION: No seed treatment is necessary, but 1 month of stratification at 40°F may improve germination, which is rapid if soils are moist and warm, delayed if they are dry or cold. Seedlings grow rapidly and produce flowers the first year. Or, divide rhizomes in the early spring and plant 2 feet apart at a depth of ½ inch. Fireweed spreads rapidly once established.

COMPANIONS: Western monkshood, pearly everlasting, Colorado columbine, leopard lily, mountain bluebells.

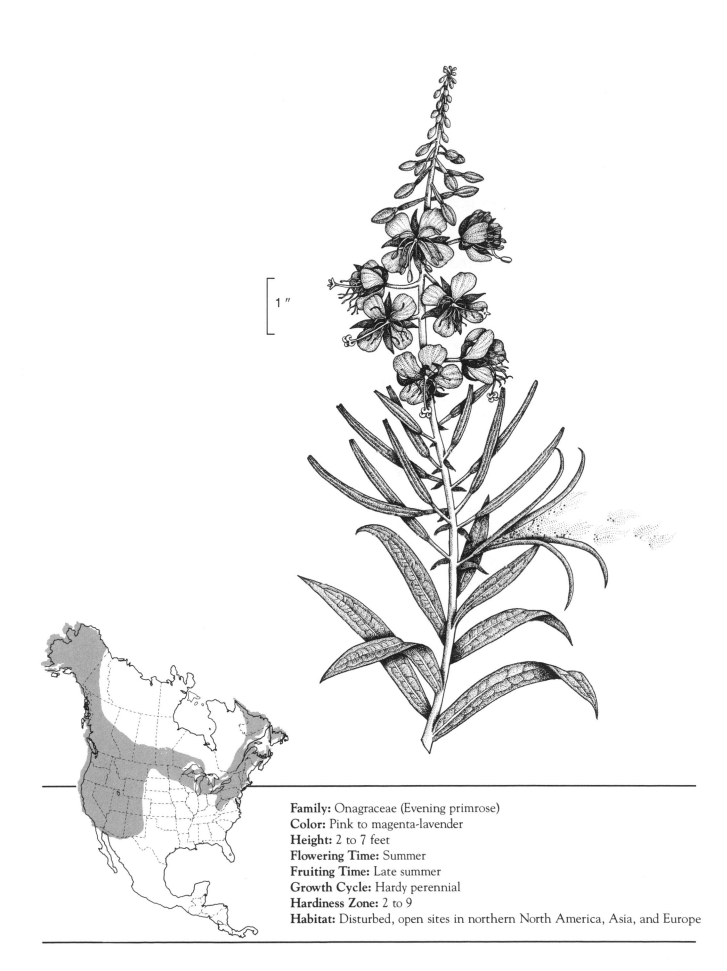

1 ″

Family: Onagraceae (Evening primrose)
Color: Pink to magenta-lavender
Height: 2 to 7 feet
Flowering Time: Summer
Fruiting Time: Late summer
Growth Cycle: Hardy perennial
Hardiness Zone: 2 to 9
Habitat: Disturbed, open sites in northern North America, Asia, and Europe

FIREWEED *(Epilobium angustifolium)*

113

BITTERROOT

While exploring the Louisiana Purchase in 1806, Captain Meriwether Lewis collected a specimen of this plant at the mouth of Lolo Creek near the present site of Missoula, Montana. Several years later Bernard McMahon, a Philadelphia horticulturist and seed merchant, planted the dried specimen and reported that it returned to life, inspiring the species name, Latin for "restored to life." Despite the common name the fleshy taproots of young plants have a ricelike flavor and were both eaten and used as a cure for sore throats by Native Americans. During mid-summer, bitterroot is dormant and hidden below the ground. In late summer the orange, carrotlike root comes to life, and many succulent, 1–3-inch-long leaves appear in clumps at the soil surface, remaining green over the winter and disappearing in the spring. As spring snows recede, 1 to several spectacular flowers appear on a short (4–6-inch) stem in the center of a rosette of leaves. The 4 to 9 flat, petallike sepals and 12 to 18 petals range in color from deep rose to pink-streaked to white. In the center of the 2-inch-wide flower are numerous stamens and a single ovary with a many-branched style. Individual flowers remain open for several days but wither once they are pollinated, usually by bees. The fruit is a papery ¼-inch capsule with many tiny, black, shiny seeds. By the time it has ripened in late spring, little of the plant is visible above ground. Bitterroot has recently been discovered at several sites east of the Continental Divide in Alberta, perhaps originating from seeds carried by the Kutenai. These Native Americans may have traded the roots during the 19th century, deeming a grain-sackful to be a fair trade for a horse.

CULTURE: Bitterroot is an ideal plant for any rock garden. While it is an extremely hardy perennial, it can be grown even in hardiness zone 10. Plant in well-drained soils in full sun. It needs moisture while flowering and when leaves are visible, but should not be watered in its summer dormancy. In humid regions, when the flower withers, cover it with an upside-down flower pot or plastic sheet to reduce the amount of rainwater penetrating the soil, and remove the covering in the late summer. If using a greenhouse, keep the plants dry from mid-spring to fall, then water sparingly until flowers appear.

PROPAGATION: Bitterroot is best propagated by seed, although the root can tolerate division and rough handling. Stratification at 33 °F for 3 months, though not necessary, greatly enhances germination. In the fall, plant the seeds ¼ inch deep in the desired location or in deep flats filled with coarse, gravelly sand. The seedlings have 2 fleshy cotyledons and will develop a few more small leaves and a 3–4-inch taproot the first growing season. When the leaves wither, transplant the root to a permanent location with the buds barely above the soil surface. By the third growing season the root system will be well developed and the plants may flower.

COMPANIONS: Old-man-of-the-mountain, sulfur-flowered eriogonum, tufted evening primrose, scarlet gilia.

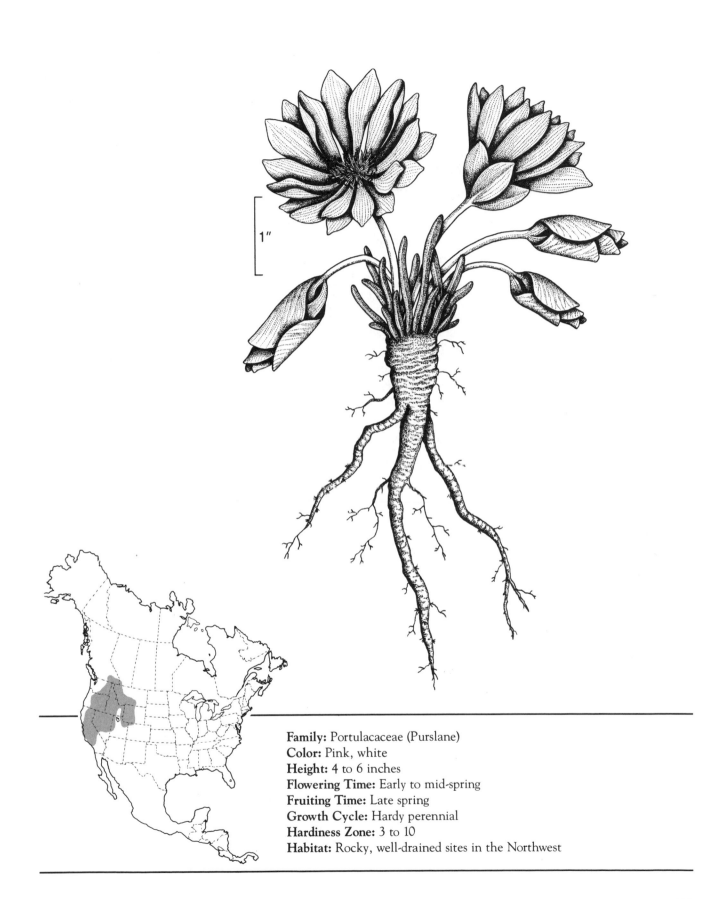

1"

Family: Portulacaceae (Purslane)
Color: Pink, white
Height: 4 to 6 inches
Flowering Time: Early to mid-spring
Fruiting Time: Late spring
Growth Cycle: Hardy perennial
Hardiness Zone: 3 to 10
Habitat: Rocky, well-drained sites in the Northwest

BITTERROOT *(Lewisia rediviva)*

YELLOW FAWN LILY

Erythronium grandiflorum

(Glacier lily, snow lily, lamb's tongue, fawn lily)

This hardy perennial, flowering as mountain snows recede, is one of the earliest wildflowers, thanks to winter bud development on its underground shoots. Flowering starts in early spring at low elevations and continues into the summer at high elevations. A 1–2-foot scape arises from between the pair of fleshy green 4–8-inch basal leaves, bearing 1 to 5 very bright yellow, nodding, 2-inch flowers that partially close at night and in cold weather. The identical sepals and petals bend back fully, exposing the white, 3-lobed stigma and the 6 long stamens arranged in 2 whorls. The large yellow, red, or white anthers on the outer whorl open immediately and those on the inner whorl open the next day. Bumblebees and other bees rapidly collect the pollen — removing about 75 percent of it in about 30 seconds — and search out the sweet nectar produced by the nectaries at the base of the ovary. The fruit, an oval, 3-sided capsule up to 1 inch long, matures two months after flowering, shaking its seeds to the ground. The root system is a slender corm about 2 inches long at maturity, grows at a depth of 3–6 inches, and produces new offsets if injured. There are two varieties of yellow fawn lily. The more widespread *grandiflorum* has yellow inch-long flowers and capsules 1¼ inches long, while variety *candidum* has white 1½-inch-long flowers and 1¾-inch-long capsules, and grows only between eastern Washington and western Montana. Native Americans used the corms as food or crushed them for a poultice to treat boils.

CULTURE: It is hard to maintain this species in soils that dry out during the summer. Moist but well-drained soils and partial shade to full sun are ideal. This hardy perennial grows best in soils that are slightly acid (pH 5-6.5) and rich in organic matter, with additions of compost and overwintering mulch left in place during the spring.

PROPAGATION: Yellow fawn lily is not considered a "commercially viable" species. Propagate it from seed instead of purchasing corms, unless you can verify that a nursery has propagated rather than collected plants. Stratify freshly collected seeds (40°F for 3½–4 months) or immediately plant the seeds ¼ inch deep in a flat filled with a mixture of compost and sand, keep the soil moist, and leave the flat out over winter to chill the seeds properly. A single leaf will emerge in the spring. Keep the developing plants shaded and moist in the flats or nursery beds for the first year and then transplant the corms 3 inches deep and 5 inches apart in permanent locations in the fall. In 2 to 4 years the plants will develop a second leaf and reach flowering size. Once established, yellow fawn lilies will self-seed in moist, humus-rich soil.

COMPANIONS: Colorado columbine, bunchberry, sky pilot, mountain bluebells.

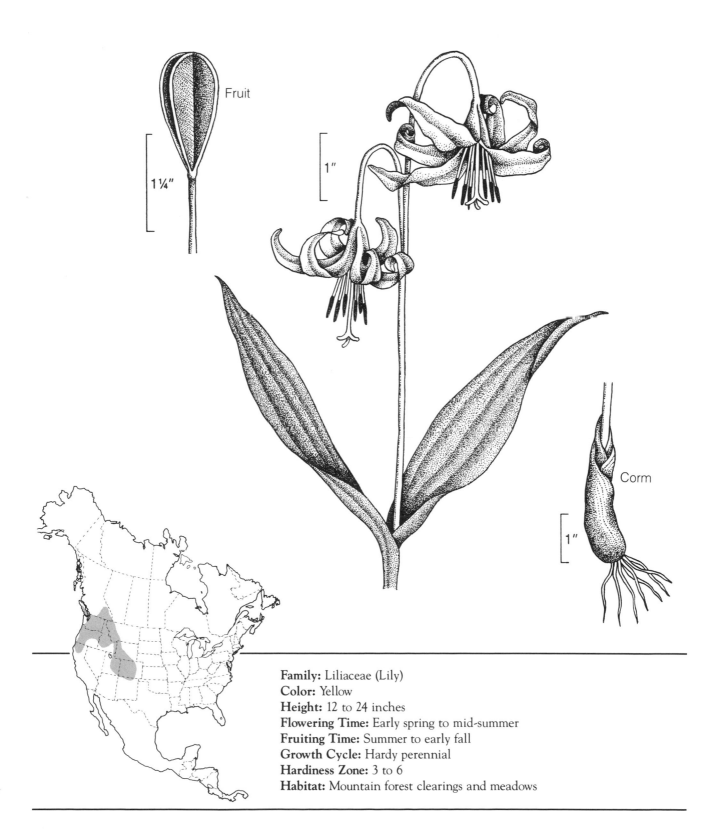

Fruit

1¼"

1"

1"

Corm

Family: Liliaceae (Lily)
Color: Yellow
Height: 12 to 24 inches
Flowering Time: Early spring to mid-summer
Fruiting Time: Summer to early fall
Growth Cycle: Hardy perennial
Hardiness Zone: 3 to 6
Habitat: Mountain forest clearings and meadows

YELLOW FAWN LILY *(Erythronium grandiflorum)*

OREGON GRAPE

Mahonia repens
(Berberis repens)

(Creeping hollygrape, creeping barberry, *mahonia rampant, yerba de sangre*)

This sprawling, woody plant is named after Bernard McMahon, the horticulturist who propagated many seeds from the Lewis & Clark expedition. Mahonia is frequently listed as Berberis, the genus of barberries, but is distinguished by its spineless stems and pinnately compound evergreen leaves. The creeping underground stems send up shoots usually under a foot in height. During the summer the 3 to 7 hollylike, 1–1½-inch leaflets are dull blue-green above and gray-green below, but usually turn red in autumn and darken over winter. Dense 1–3-inch clusters of ¼-inch yellow flowers appear at the ends of branches in the spring, blooming first in the Pacific Northwest and later in the Rockies. On each flower 6 round-tipped petallike sepals and 6 petals with clefted tips surround a single pistil with a superior ovary, capped by a dimpled, circular stigma. Six stamens spring up when the petals and sepals are touched by solitary bees searching for nectar hidden in glands at the bases of petals. Dark blue-purple ¼-inch berries, covered with a light blue blush and containing a single seed, are produced by mid-summer, about a month after flowering. Not only do birds and mammals eat the fruits and disperse the seeds, but Native Americans, who actively traded the tart berries, used them and the yellow, spreading roots and inner bark for medicinal purposes. Oregon grape is a favorite of white-tail deer and cattle in late summer.

CULTURE: Oregon grape needs well-drained soil and grows best where organic matter is abundant. It tolerates soil pH of 4.5-7.5, but 5.5-7.0 is ideal. In partial shade it sprawls rapidly; in full sun, it grows slowly in a dense, compact form and has lighter green leaves. Protect the foliage during the winter from burns by intense sun and high winds. It is also sensitive to salt, so do not plant it along the immediate coast or near roads that are salted during the winter. An excellent ground cover for controlling erosion on banks, Oregon grape is both relatively drought tolerant and resistant to the black stem rust of wheat. It can be used as a container plant indoors or out.

PROPAGATION: Oregon grape can be propagated from seed, divisions, or cuttings. Remove the seeds from the ripe berries to reduce chances of molding and to hasten germination. Stratify the seeds for at least 3 months at 40°F in damp peat moss, or immediately plant the seeds ¼ inch deep in a cool spot outdoors and cover them with a thin layer of mulch. Germination usually occurs the following spring as the seed coat is pushed out of the ground by the elongating shoot. Some seeds will germinate after the second winter. Oregon grape is also easily propagated by root divisions made in the spring or cuttings of green twigs made in the early summer. Plant divisions or rooted cuttings a foot apart and keep them moist, but not wet, until reestablished.

COMPANIONS: Harebell, Colorado columbine, yellow fawn lily, scarlet gilia.

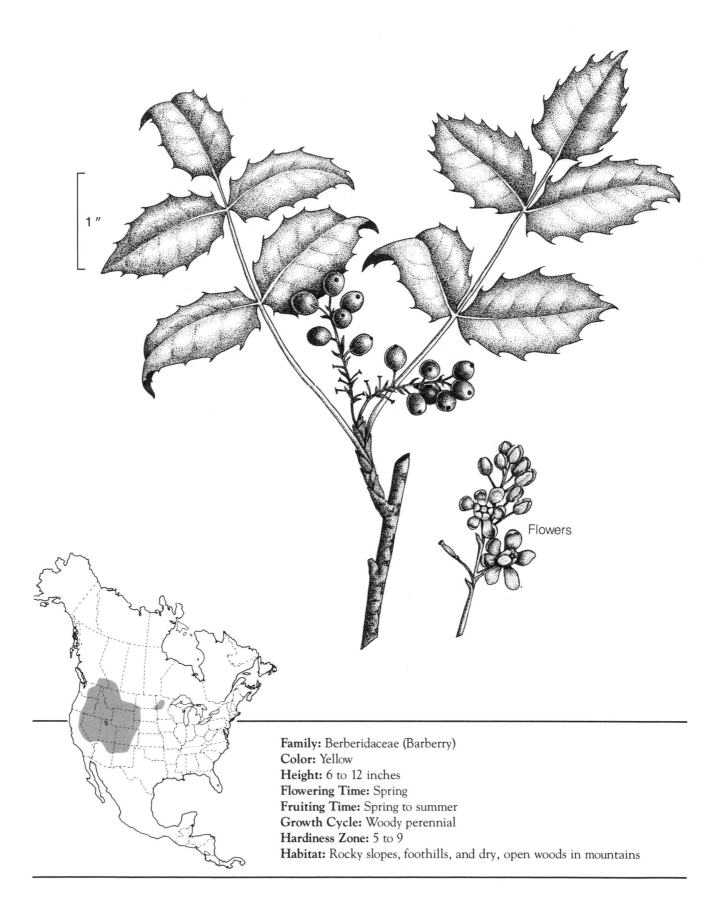

Flowers

Family: Berberidaceae (Barberry)
Color: Yellow
Height: 6 to 12 inches
Flowering Time: Spring
Fruiting Time: Spring to summer
Growth Cycle: Woody perennial
Hardiness Zone: 5 to 9
Habitat: Rocky slopes, foothills, and dry, open woods in mountains

OREGON GRAPE *(Mahonia repens)*

MOUNTAIN BLUEBELLS

Mertensia ciliata

(Chiming bells)

The flower buds of this western montane perennial start out pink, but produce pendant clusters of sky blue flowers from spring snow melt-off to mid-summer. Typically, several 1–3-foot stems emerge in a clump from the branched, woody roots. The smooth, veiny, 2–4-inch leaves, crowded along the hollow stems, have small hairs along their edges and pointed tips, described by the Latin name *ciliata.* The lowest leaves have distinct petioles, while the upper ones are attached directly to the stem. The succulent leaves tend to wilt when it is droughty or even in the noonday sun. An arched cluster of clear blue ¾-inch tubular flowers blooms from tip to base. Five stamens are attached to the inside of the pendant tubular corolla with a flaring 5-lobed bell at its opening, protecting them from rain. The anthers shed their pollen for the first 2 days after the corolla opens. Each section of the 4-part ovary inside the corolla contains a single ovule. The long style that extends beyond the mouth of the corolla ends in a stigma is that is receptive for 4 to 5 days. A mild fragrance and sweet nectar are produced by the nectaries below the ovary. Mountain bluebells is pollinated primarily by worker bumblebees, both long-tongued and short-tongued species. Long-tongued species can reach the nectar directly; short-tongued species either collect pollen by rapidly beating their wings to shake it loose, or rob nectar by chewing holes in the petal tube near the short, hairy, 5-part calyx. About 5 weeks after a flower opens, it produces 4 rough, leathery, wrinkled nutlet fruits. Mountain bluebells' root crowns and rhizomes spread over time, forming extensive patches.

CULTURE: Mountain bluebells thrives in semi-shade, even in sites with little full sun, but will grow happily in wet meadows. It needs damp soils with constant moisture during the growing season, and will tolerate saturated soils. Its size and the length of its flowering season are influenced by the amount of soil moisture. Loams and sandy loams of pH 5.5-7.0 are ideal. Be sure to provide good air circulation to prevent mildew diseases. Plants from high-elevation sites are typically shorter than those of lower elevations. Yellow-bellied marmots eat leaves, as do sheep, so fencing may be necessary.

PROPAGATION: Mountain bluebells propagates itself naturally, mostly by extension of its rhizomes. Divide the rhizomes in the spring and plant 1 inch deep, about a foot apart. It can also be propagated from seed. Fresh seed is dormant, but the dormancy is lost with age. Seed scarification enhances germination. Rub gently between sheets of medium-grit sandpaper to scratch the seed coat, and plant ¼ inch deep in the desired locations. Germination is rapid in the spring as the soil temperature nears 70°F, but will also occur at lower temperatures.

COMPANIONS: Yellow fawn lily, bunchberry, elephantheads, Washington lupine.

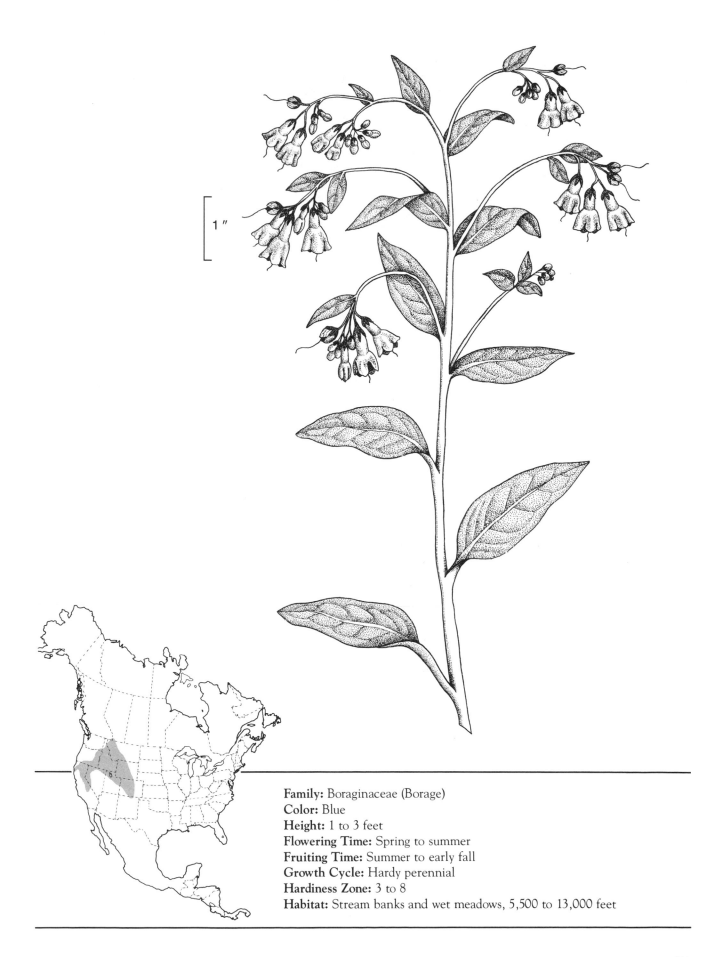

Family: Boraginaceae (Borage)
Color: Blue
Height: 1 to 3 feet
Flowering Time: Spring to summer
Fruiting Time: Summer to early fall
Growth Cycle: Hardy perennial
Hardiness Zone: 3 to 8
Habitat: Stream banks and wet meadows, 5,500 to 13,000 feet

MOUNTAIN BLUEBELLS *(Mertensia ciliata)*

PLATTE RIVER PENSTEMON *Penstemon cyananthus*

(Wasatch penstemon)

The Platte River in Wyoming and the Wasatch Mountains in Utah have both given their names to this lovely blue-violet penstemon. The name penstemon is derived from the 5 stamens of plants in this genus, only 4 of which are fertile. The fifth, golden stamen is typically quite hairy and gives the penstemon another common name, "beardtongue." The Platte River penstemon has erect, smooth, 1–2-foot stems with pairs of clasping, lance-shaped, 1–4-inch leaves. Densely clustered rings of bright blue to blue-violet flowers are borne at the top of the stem. Each of the inch-long, smooth, tubular flowers has a 2-lobed upper lip and a 3-lobed lower lip that serves as a landing pad for the bees that pollinate it. The capsular fruit splits open when it is ripe to reveal many small, irregularly angled seeds.

CULTURE:
Penstemons should be grown in sunny, open locations with soils that are moist to dry, but very well drained. Sandy loam soils are ideal and heavy soils should be lightened by the addition of sand and organic matter. Once established, this hardy perennial is relatively drought resistant and should not be overwatered because of possible root rot and mildew problems. Platte River penstemon can be grown in hardiness zones 3-6.

PROPAGATION:
While Platte River penstemon can be propagated by stem cuttings and root divisions, propagation by seed is the preferred method. Seeds do not require chilling treatment, but moist stratification for several months at 40°F significantly enhances germination. Seeds also germinate better when exposed to light, so barely scratch them into the surface of the soil and keep moist until the seedlings become established. Alternatively, start seeds indoors in the early spring in flats or peat pots and transplant outdoors when danger of frost is past. These plants may actually bloom by the end of the first year, although flowering in the second year is more common. Root divisions can be made in late fall, being sure that each division has at least one shoot bud. Plant the segments with the bud just at the soil surface. Softwood cuttings can also be made in the summer from non-flowering shoots. A 6–7-inch cutting should be planted 3 inches deep in sharp sand, and kept moist, but not wet, until the roots develop. Plant the dormant rootstock in the late fall with the newly formed buds just at the ground surface.

COMPANIONS:
Rocky Mountain penstemon, blue flax, tufted evening primrose, mule's ears, scarlet gilia.

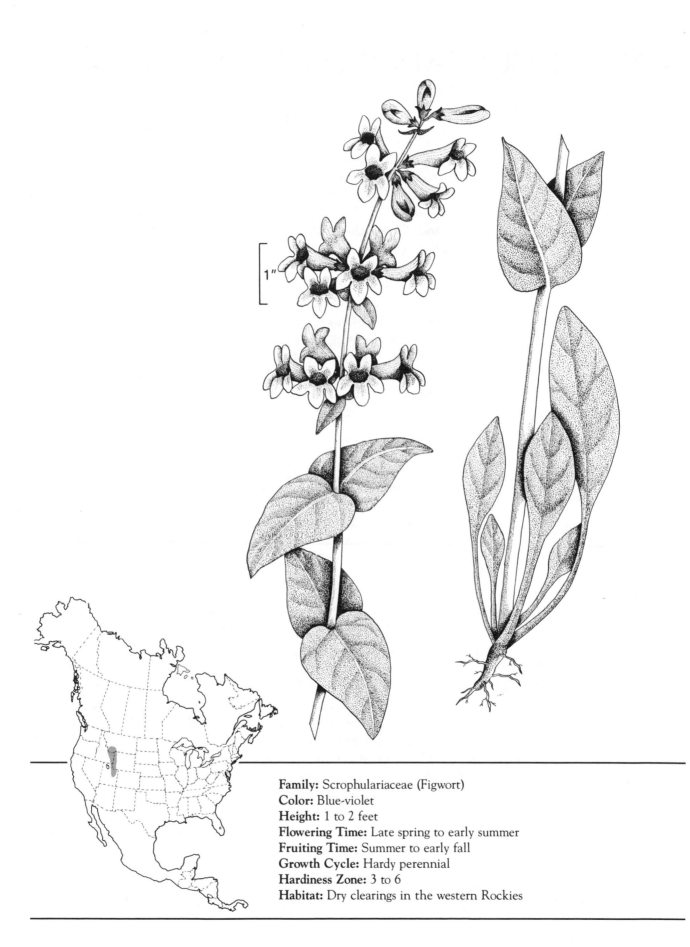

Family: Scrophulariaceae (Figwort)
Color: Blue-violet
Height: 1 to 2 feet
Flowering Time: Late spring to early summer
Fruiting Time: Summer to early fall
Growth Cycle: Hardy perennial
Hardiness Zone: 3 to 6
Habitat: Dry clearings in the western Rockies

PLATTE RIVER PENSTEMON (*Penstemon cyananthus*)

ROCKY MOUNTAIN PENSTEMON *Penstemon strictus*

(Porch penstemon)

True to its name, this medium-sized penstemon is a plant of the western side of the Continental Divide. Rocky Mountain penstemon stands 1–2½ feet high, with royal blue to purple flowers on one side of the upper half of the stem. Flowers of this species vary in size from ¾–1¾ inches long. The considerable variation in flower size and shape is the product of the evolutionary interplay between populations of Rocky Mountain penstemon and their local pollinating insects. The 2 lobes of the tubular flower's upper lip project forward like a visor over the lower lip's 3 deeply cleft, downwardly bent lobes, which serve as a landing platform for bee pollinators. The resemblance of the upper lip to a roof and the lower lip to steps is the origin of the common name "porch penstemon." The 4 fertile stamens, their anthers covered by long, tangled hairs, give a fuzzy appearance to the inside of the flower's throat. The fifth, sterile stamen is usually heavily bearded, but sometimes hairless. Not only do the flowers vary, but the pairs of leaves range from narrow and grasslike to rather broad and lance-shaped. The leaves are a deeper green than the stem, which is covered with a whitish, waxy coating.

CULTURE: Rocky Mountain penstemon should be planted in full sun to light shade on well-drained, sandy, gravelly, or stony soils. Moisture is essential for young plants to become established, but the mature plants are quite drought tolerant and do better in dryer soils — although during extreme dry spells flowering is reduced. In regions with hot summer temperatures, they do better if lightly shaded from the noon-time sun.

PROPAGATION: Propagation by either root divisions or seed is successful, but seeds are usually used. Plant the seeds in the fall after the fruits are fully mature. Seed germination is enhanced by a moist chilling treatment (2–3 months at 40°F). The seeds also germinate better when exposed to light, so barely scratch them into the surface of the soil and keep moist until the seedlings become established. Generally seeds germinate after 1 to 2 weeks of temperatures above 60°F. Some plants from seed may bloom during the first year, and most will the second. Make root divisions in the early spring, being sure that each division has at least one bud. Plant the segments 1–2 feet apart with the bud just at the ground surface. In time, several stems will emerge from the rootstock and the clumps can be divided again.

COMPANIONS: Platte River penstemon, blue flax, tufted evening primrose, mule's ears, scarlet gilia.

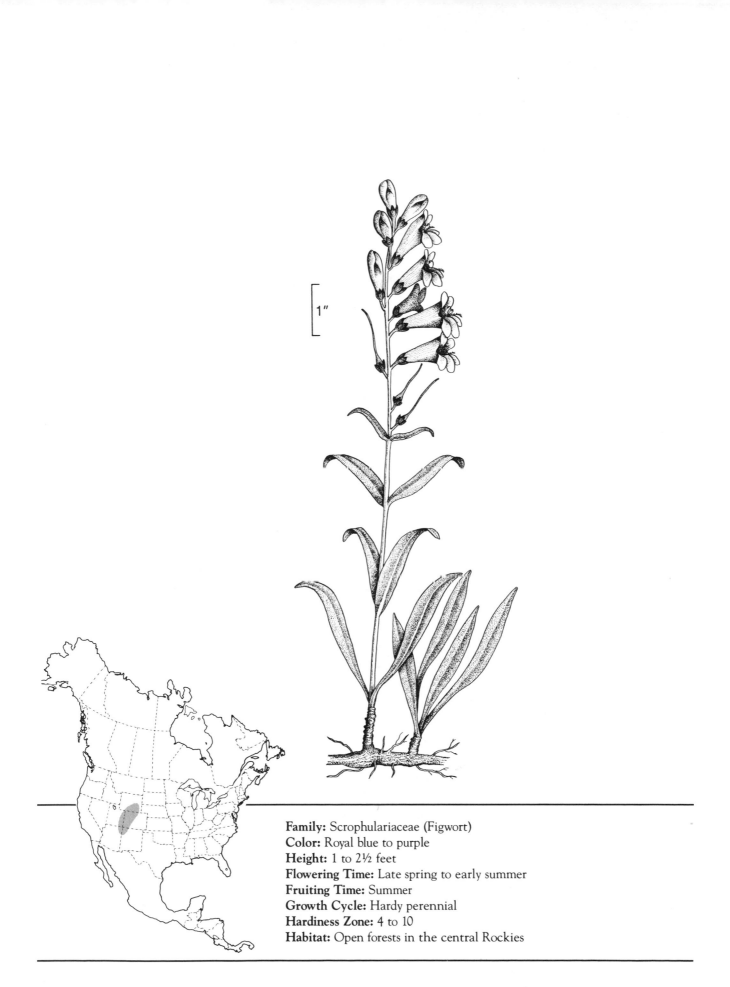

Family: Scrophulariaceae (Figwort)
Color: Royal blue to purple
Height: 1 to 2½ feet
Flowering Time: Late spring to early summer
Fruiting Time: Summer
Growth Cycle: Hardy perennial
Hardiness Zone: 4 to 10
Habitat: Open forests in the central Rockies

ROCKY MOUNTAIN PENSTEMON *(Penstemon strictus)*

ALPINE SPECIES

Few people have the opportunity to garden above the timberline from 10,000 to 14,000 feet or higher. You do not need to reproduce an environment of high winds, constant frost hazard, and intense sunlight, however, to grow alpine wildflowers successfully at a lower elevation, as long as the garden is not too hot during the summer.

Alpine species are adapted to very short growing seasons by having a burst of growth and flowering just as the winter snows are melting. The deeper the winter snow pack, the later the growing season starts, but more moisture is available for plant growth.

An enormous diversity of wildflowers thrives in the extreme environment of an alpine garden. A few montane wildflowers like **mountain bluebells** (*Mertensia ciliata*) make their way to the tops of mountains, but low-growing plants like **alpine bluebells** (*M. alpina*) are more common above timberline.

A veritable palette of color is available to the alpine gardener, with the clear blues of the **alpine forget-me-not** (*Eritrichum aretioides*) and **delicate Jacob's ladder** (*Polemonium delicatum*) complementing those of harebell and sky pilot. The pinnate-leaf daisy (*Erigeron pinnatisectus*), with its attractive fernlike leaves, has large flower heads with a dense ring of narrow magenta-lavender ray flowers surrounding the golden disk flowers at the center. The stonecrop family includes some alpine members with red flowers like **Queens crown** (*Clementsia rhodantha*) and **Kings crown** (*Rhodiola integrifolia*) and others with yellow flowers like **yellow stonecrop** (*Sedum lanceolatum*). **Alpine spring beauty** (*Claytonia megarhiza*) flowers are a pure white with delicate pink lines running from the tips to the bases of the petals, while **moss campion** (*Silene acaulis*) forms a mosslike mat from which arise bright pink flowers with notched tips.

The flowers of alpine phlox species generally range from white to light pink or pale blue. **Spreading phlox** (*Phlox difusa*) of the Sierra Nevada and Cascades, **tufted phlox** (*P. caespitosa*) of the Rockies, and the **carpet phlox** (*P. hoodii*) found

Alpine garden.

A. Elephantheads
B. Harebell
C. Sky pilot
D. Sulfur-flowered eriogonum
E. Old-man-of-the-mountain
F. Mountain dryas

at lower elevations in the Columbia Plateau all make excellent low-growing additions to rock gardens.

Woody plants have trouble growing in the harsh, windswept alpine environment, and those that survive either grow in mats or look more like bonsai than erect trees and shrubs. One of the most attractive shrubs growing above timberline is **alpine laurel** (*Kalmia microphylla*) with small, evergreen leaves and clusters of bright pink, bowl-shaped flowers. Trees are few, but **white-bark pine** (*Pinus albicaulis*) and **bristlecone pine** (*P. aristata*) are two of the highest-elevation tree species, growing in the open woodlands in the upper montane zone.

HAREBELL

Campanula rotundifolia

(Bluebell of Scotland, Scotch bellflower, *campanule à feuilles rondes*)

Although the harebell is sometimes called "bluebell of Scotland," this variable perennial's range encircles the globe in the Northern Hemisphere. While the *rotundifolia* part of this wildflower's Latin name means "round leaves," only the leaves at the very base of the stem are round, and they usually wither before flowering starts. Most of the leaves are threadlike and about 3 inches long, and are thought to be the origin of the common name, a Scottish corruption of "hairbell." One to several nodding flowers hang from threadlike pedicles extending from the 6–24-inch-high unbranched or sparingly branched stems. Plants at lower elevations tend to be taller with more flowers. Each flower is like a little bell (*campanula* in Latin) ½–1 inch across with 5 pointed corolla lobes that curve outward slightly. The flowers range from pale blue to sky blue to lavender, generally becoming lighter toward the base. The 5 calyx lobes have elongated awl-shaped points. The long flowering season typically runs from June to September or later. As the flowers open the anthers on the 5 lavender stamens contain ripe pollen. This is rapidly removed by honeybees and beeflies seeking the nectar contained within the ringlike nectary at the base of the style. Bristles on the style meanwhile collect pollen from the bodies of the insect visitors. The flower becomes receptive to pollen when the 3 stigma lobes split and curl back, sometimes touching the anthers, although pollen is incapable of fertilizing the ovules of the same flower. The fruit, a nodding top-shaped capsule, opens by pores at its base, releasing the tiny, flat, shiny, chestnut brown seeds. Harebell spreads vigorously over time, new shoots arising from the slender, much-branched rhizome rootstocks.

CULTURE: Harebell is a wonderfully versatile wildflower in sun or light shade. No rock garden is complete without it, but it can also be used in meadow gardens. Well-drained, sandy to gravelly soils of near-neutral pH are ideal for its cultivation. While harebell is relatively drought tolerant, young plants benefit from ample but not excessive moisture. This species can become rampant, but if planted in shallow soils with no additional fertilizers it is well behaved.

PROPAGATION: Harebell is quite easy to grow from seed. No treatment is necessary, but seeds may need light for best germination, so plant them shallowly on the soil surface, raking them in lightly. Germination typically takes a week or two. Once established, harebell tends to self-sow freely and may even need weeding. Roots can be divided early in the spring, and stem cuttings, taken with a bit of rootstock, can be made before flowering commences. Place divisions ½ inch deep and 12-18 inches apart.

COMPANIONS: Sulfur-flowered eriogonum, sky pilot, Rocky Mountain penstemon, Platte River penstemon.

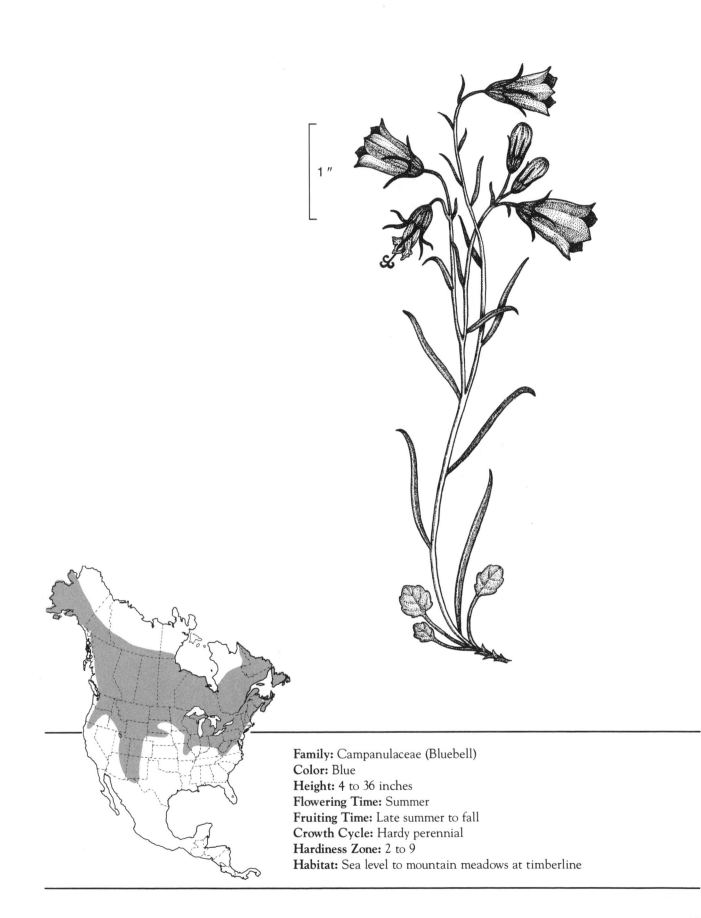

Family: Campanulaceae (Bluebell)
Color: Blue
Height: 4 to 36 inches
Flowering Time: Summer
Fruiting Time: Late summer to fall
Crowth Cycle: Hardy perennial
Hardiness Zone: 2 to 9
Habitat: Sea level to mountain meadows at timberline

1 ″

HAREBELL (*Campanula rotundifolia*)

MOUNTAIN DRYAS

Dryas octopetala
(Dryas hookeriana)

(White mountain avens, Mountain dryad)

Although *dryas* is Greek for wood nymph, this wildflower grows above the timberlines of mountains in western North America, Asia, and Europe. Mountain dryas is a slow-growing perennial with woody stems forming mats up to 3 feet across and usually less than 1 foot high. In Europe some of these mats have been estimated to be more than 100 years old. The mats appear to be a mass of inch-long, oval, leathery evergreen leaves with rounded teeth along their curled edges. The undersides of the leaves are silvery and the leaf base clasps the woody stem. The leaves are actually only "wintergreen": that is, they remain green during the winter but deteriorate rapidly as new leaves are produced in the spring. The leaves have high rates of photosynthesis, an important adaptation in a habitat with a very short growing season. North America has at least two subspecies. The larger-leaved, less hairy *alaskensis* subspecies is found in the protection of snowbanks where the soils are moist and nutrient-rich but the growing season is very short. The smaller-leaved, hairier *octopetala* subspecies grows in exposed, dry, rocky fellfields, and flowers about 10 days earlier. Single white 1½-inch flowers looking like 8-to-10-petaled miniature roses are borne atop 2–8-inch-high stems. The flowers have 8 to 10 narrow, pointed, hairy sepals and many stamens and pistils. The fluffy, feathery, inch-long, seedlike fruits mature in early summer.

CULTURE: Mountain dryas is a plant of cool environments, and while it grows from hardiness zones 8 to 1, high summer temperatures (above 80°F) are more of a limitation than cold winters are. It grows best where some snow cover protects it from dry winter winds. On exposed sites the plants will benefit from a layer of mulch during the winter, removed in the early spring. This sun-loving wildflower is most abundant on limestone outcrops but tolerates more acidic garden conditions, growing at soil pH ranging 5.5-7.5. Mountain dryas's preference for well-drained, gravelly-sandy soils makes it an ideal plant for the rock garden as long as the site is not too dry or exposed to summer winds. It does not respond to fertilizers. Leaf miners may be a periodic problem, but are usually not fatal.

PROPAGATION: Mountain dryas can be propagated by seeds or root divisions. Cold, moist stratification of seeds for several months substantially increases germination; or plant fresh seeds ¼–⅓ inch deep in the desired locations and let cold winter temperatures stratify them naturally. The seeds germinate rapidly, usually within a week if soil is kept moist, but the plants then take 3 years to flower. Mountain dryas is also easily propagated by dividing the woody rootstock or portions of the horizontal, creeping stem with new roots. Make the divisions in the early spring and plant them 8–12 inches apart.

COMPANIONS: Old-man-of-the-mountain, sky pilot, bitterroot, blue flax, sulfur-flowered eriogonum.

Family: Rosaceae (Rose)
Color: White
Height: 2 to 8 inches
Flowering Time: Late spring
Fruiting Time: Early summer
Growth Cycle: Hardy perennial
Hardiness Zone: 1 to 8
Habitat: Alpine tundra to arctic North America and Europe

MOUNTAIN DRYAS (*Dryas octopetala*)

SULFUR-FLOWERED ERIOGONUM *Eriogonum umbellatum*

(Sulfur flower, sulfur-flowered buckwheat)

Although sulfur-flowered eriogonum can be found growing near sea level in some places in the Northwest, its cushions of sulfur-yellow flowers are most spectacular high in the Sierra Nevada and Rocky Mountains, where they frequently trap the seeds of other plants to form natural rock gardens. This perennial forms 4–12-inch-high mounds of gray-green, spatula-shaped, 1½-inch-long leaves, which have wooly undersides and are attached to the tips of creeping woody stems. Foothigh, leafless, hairy flowering scapes arise out of the mats in late spring through mid-summer, bearing round, 2–4-inch clusters of 20 to 30 bright yellow flowers above whorls of small leafy bracts. Each of the small (¼-inch) flowers has 6 bright yellow to cream petallike parts, 9 stamens, and a triangular 1-celled ovary with 3 styles. The flowers, which are everlasting if properly dried, turn reddish with age, and then maroon or brown as the 3-sided seedlike fruits, with tufts of hair and 3 persistent styles at the top, mature. Bees find the flowers' sweet nectar irresistible, as do many species of butterflies. While *E. umbellatum* is quite abundant in the Pacific Northwest and Rocky Mountain regions, among its 25 recognized varieties and subspecies are several that are rare or found only in local areas. Variety *minus* is limited to the San Gabriel Mountains of southern California, variety *aridum* appears to be relatively scarce even where it grows between the San Bernardino Mountains and the east slope of the Sierra Nevada, and the rare and endangered variety *torreyanum* grows only from Modoc to Placer counties in California.

CULTURE: Sulfur-flowered eriogonum grows best in dry, sunny locations with well-drained soils. Although it is included here with alpine plants, it will grow from sea level to above timberline. Once established, this wildflower is exceedingly drought tolerant, but a bit of extra moisture during the summer will prolong its flowering season. Sulfur-flowered eriogonum usually is found growing on limestone soils and does best in the garden in soils with pH 6.5-8. It can be used as a ground cover if planted densely.

PROPAGATION: Propagate only by seed since it is nearly impossible to transplant or divide the long taproots of mature plants. No seed treatment is necessary, but 3-month stratification may improve germination. Plant seeds thickly because the percentage germinating even under the best of conditions is low. Simply rake the seeds into the surface of the soil in late summer or early fall. If started in flats, transplant to permanent locations when seedlings are small.

COMPANIONS: Bitterroot, scarlet gilia, blue flax, sky pilot, old-man-of-the-mountain.

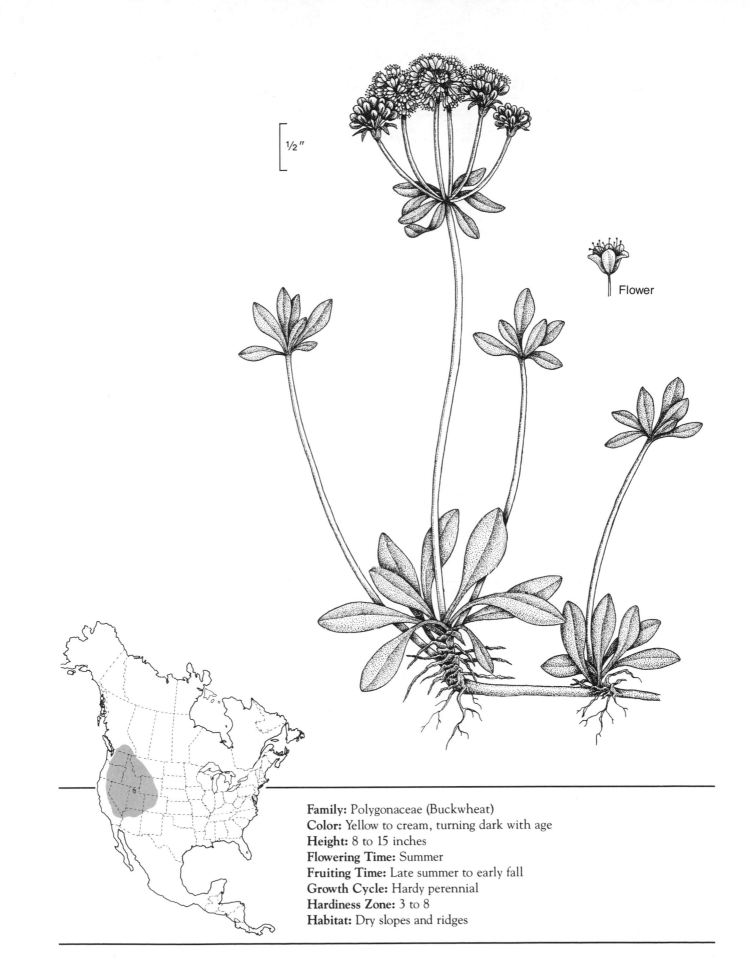

½″

Flower

Family: Polygonaceae (Buckwheat)
Color: Yellow to cream, turning dark with age
Height: 8 to 15 inches
Flowering Time: Summer
Fruiting Time: Late summer to early fall
Growth Cycle: Hardy perennial
Hardiness Zone: 3 to 8
Habitat: Dry slopes and ridges

SULFUR-FLOWERED ERIOGONUM (*Eriogonum umbellatum*)

OLD-MAN-OF-THE-MOUNTAIN *Hymenoxys grandiflora* (*Rydbergia g., Actinea g.*)

(Rydbergia, alpine sunflower, alpine goldflower, sun god)

This very hardy alpine plant is one of the showiest wildflowers of the Rockies. Out of a low mat of feathery, 3–4-inch-long leaves, covered with cottony white hairs, rise 3–4-inch sunflowerlike flower heads on stems usually less than a foot high. Often the stems are so short that the large flowers seem embedded in the foliage. The flower heads usually are found facing eastward toward the rising sun. Twenty or more inch-long ray flowers have broad, overlapping, bright yellow petals with 3 teeth at the tip, and surround the broad, domed disc densely packed with small disc flowers. The disc flowers turn from bright yellow to tan with age. Numerous wooly, leafy bracts surround the flower head. The 5-sided, conical, hairy, seedlike fruits have narrow scales at the top. Old-man-of-the-mountain's alternate common name and its former genus name, *Rydbergia*, are in honor of Per Axel Rydberg, a botanist who made extensive surveys of the Rocky Mountains and Great Plains for the U.S. Department of Agriculture and the New York Botanical Garden in the late 19th and early 20th centuries.

CULTURE: Old-man-of-the-mountain is a plant of the alpine tundra and high meadows. It requires full sunlight and well-drained soils that are moist during the growing season. Preferring gravelly, limestone-rich soils (pH 6.0-7.5), this hardy perennial is ideal for rock gardens in hardiness zone 4 and colder. It grows best where summers are cool and dry, and if periodic moisture is sufficient the late spring to early summer flowering period can be prolonged.

PROPAGATION: Old-man-of-the-mountain is best propagated by seed. Collect the seeds in the late summer when fruits are ripe. Plant ¼ inch deep in a permanent location or in flats filled with sand or coarse soil, and leave outdoors for the winter. While stratification is not essential, the seeds, like those of most alpine plants, have enhanced springtime germination if given a moist, cold treatment. Transplant seedlings as soon as they are sturdy, so as not to interfere with the developing taproot. It takes a full year for seedlings of this biennial to reach flowering size. Some populations of old-man-of-the-mountain appear to behave as monocarpic perennials, dying abruptly after flowering, so it is a good idea to stagger plantings over several years.

COMPANIONS: Mountain dryas, sulfur-flowered eriogonum, bunchberry, bitterroot, sky pilot, harebell.

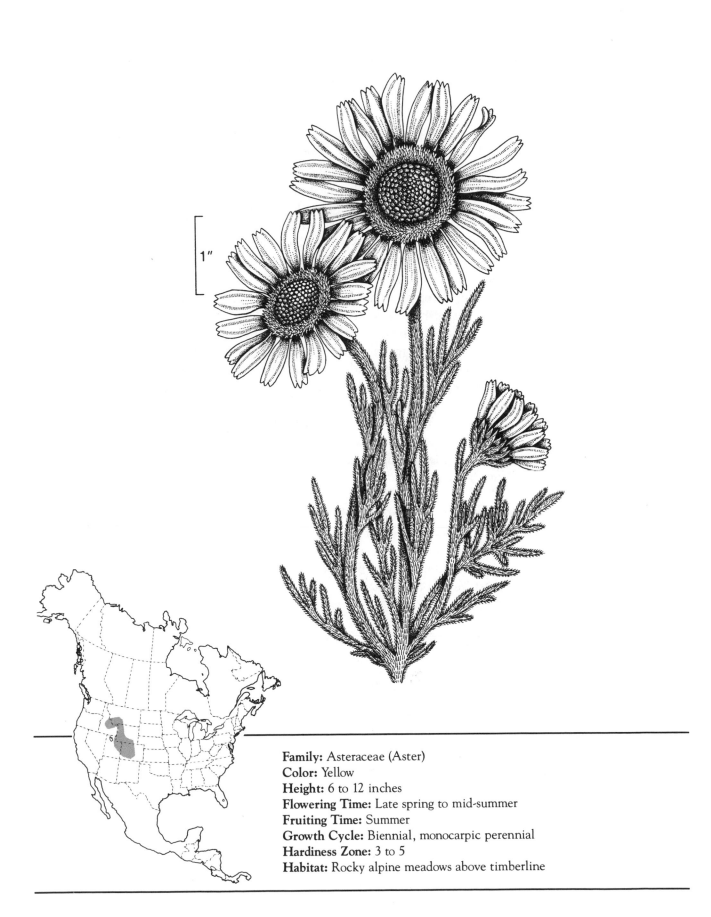

Family: Asteraceae (Aster)
Color: Yellow
Height: 6 to 12 inches
Flowering Time: Late spring to mid-summer
Fruiting Time: Summer
Growth Cycle: Biennial, monocarpic perennial
Hardiness Zone: 3 to 5
Habitat: Rocky alpine meadows above timberline

OLD-MAN-OF-THE-MOUNTAIN *(Hymenoxys grandiflora)*

ELEPHANTHEADS

Pedicularis groenlandica

(Little pink elephants, elephantella)

This hardy perennial of wet alpine meadows and boreal regions sports what might be the most fantastic flowers of any plant in North America. Each of the many flowers clustered on the 6–24-inch-high scape resembles the head of a miniature pink elephant. The elephant's dark trunk and lighter forehead are actually the flower's upper 2 lips, while the ears and the rest of the head are the lower 3 lips. The style runs the length of the trunk and the stigma projects out of the snout. The flowers bloom just as worker bumblebees, their only pollinators, emerge in the spring. Not only have the flowers evolved to fit the bumblebee's shape, but they also reflect ultraviolet light, visible to insects but not to humans. Without bumblebees elephantheads won't produce seeds, but since the flowers do not produce any nectar, pollen is the insects' only reward. As the bumblebee lands on a flower it bites the face of the flower, grasps the "ears" with its feet, and extracts pollen from the anthers in the "forehead" by rapidly vibrating its wings. Clouds of pollen are released and whatever clings to the insect's body is transferred to the next flower's stigma. The insect "grooms" the remaining pollen off its body and packs it in pollen sacs on its legs. The fruit is a ¼-inch capsule containing 1/8-inch seeds. The smooth, fernlike leaves are 2-10 inches long, have sharply toothed lobes, and are most abundant near the base of the scape. The dissected form of the leaves appears to help the plant dissipate the heat of the intense alpine sun.

CULTURE: Elephantheads is a plant of cold, wet meadows. It should be planted where summer temperatures are not excessive and soil moisture is abundant. You don't need an alpine meadow to grow this plant; it can be grown in warmer regions, but requires moisture and full sun.

PROPAGATION: Elephantheads seed requires damp stratification (40°F for 2-3 months) to ensure germination. In the fall, plant the seeds 1/8-¼ inch deep in flats containing a mixture of compost, loam, and peat moss, and leave out over the winter. Germination will start in the spring. Leave the seedlings in the flats for the first growing season and then transplant them to permanent locations when dormant in the fall.

COMPANIONS: Mountain bluebells, Washington lupine, bunchberry.

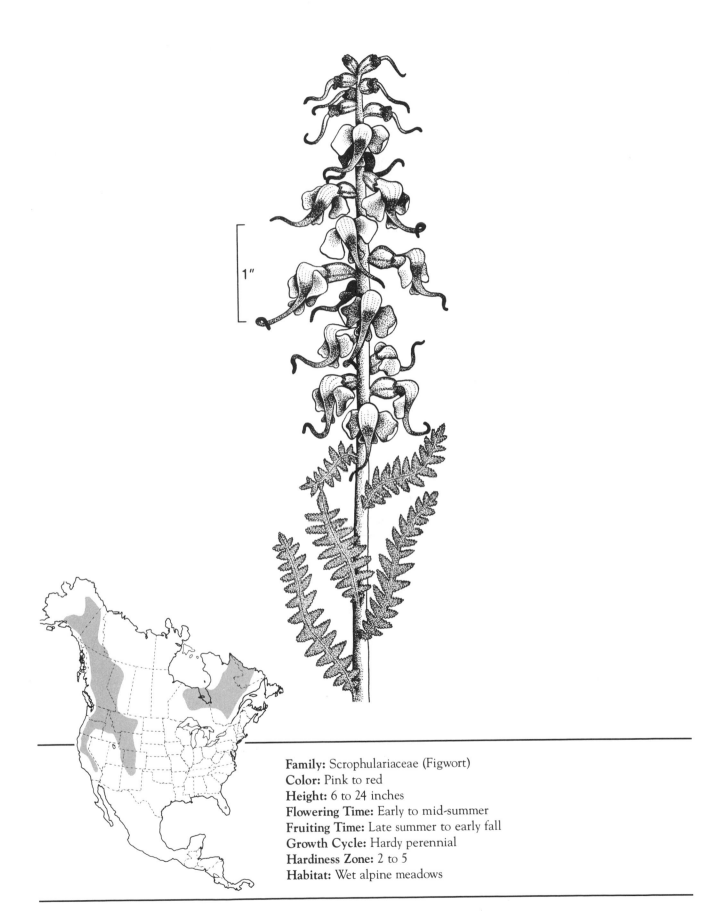

1"

Family: Scrophulariaceae (Figwort)
Color: Pink to red
Height: 6 to 24 inches
Flowering Time: Early to mid-summer
Fruiting Time: Late summer to early fall
Growth Cycle: Hardy perennial
Hardiness Zone: 2 to 5
Habitat: Wet alpine meadows

ELEPHANTHEADS (*Pedicularis groenlandica*)

SKY PILOT

Polemonium viscosum

(Skunk polemonium)

Sky pilot's clear blue flowers and attractive foliage make it one of the favorite alpine wildflowers in western gardens. It has tufts of bright green 3–6-inch leaves, most of which are subdivided into thick fernlike segments with whorls of small leaflets, although some are grasslike. Sometimes both leaf types are found on the same plant. In late spring, or in early summer at higher elevations, a 4–20-inch scape rises out of the rosette of leaves, bearing a 2–4-inch cluster of 5 to 25 half-inch, light blue or occasionally white flowers. Each has a 5-lobed trumpet-shaped corolla surrounded by a tubular calyx with 5 hairy sepal lobes. A subspecies with yellow flowers and more open clusters is found in the eastern Rockies. The attractive stamens, with bright golden-orange anthers, are attached halfway up the corolla and project from its throat. Pollen is shed from the anthers as individual flowers open, and shortly thereafter the 3-part stigma becomes receptive and remains so until the flower withers in about 4 days. Cross-pollination is needed for sky pilot to produce abundant seeds, since pollen from a flower is rarely capable of fertilizing its own ovules. Sky pilot has both skunky-smelling and sweet-scented flowers, and is pollinated both by flies attracted to the skunky odor and by moths and bumblebees attracted to the sweeter fragrance. Ants also visit sky pilot flowers and "steal" the nectar, either by crawling into the flower or by chewing a hole through the corolla to drink from the nectaries without pollinating the flower. In the process they often damage the style and ovary, so where ant activity is high seed set is frequently reduced. Ants appear to be repelled by sky pilot's skunky odor and show a decided preference for the sweeter-smelling flowers.

CULTURE: Sky pilot grows best on rocky, well-drained soils in full sun to very light shade, but needs periodic moisture during the growing season. In dry years it produces few flowers on straggly stems, while in moist years it produces more erect, robust stems with numerous flowers in heads. Ant damage can be controlled with tanglefoot.

PROPAGATION: Propagate sky pilot from seed. Cold, moist stratification enhances germination, so store fresh seeds at 40°F for 2 to 3 months and then plant indoors in flats in the early spring, or later outdoors in the desired locations when the soil can be worked. Plant fresh seeds in late summer or fall by gently scratching them into the surface of the soil. Do not plant seeds deeply, as germination is stimulated by light. The seeds take about 2 weeks to germinate in the spring after the soils have warmed. Keep seedlings moist, but not wet, until young plants are established.

COMPANIONS: Mountain dryas, old-man-of-the-mountain, sulfur-flowered eriogonum.

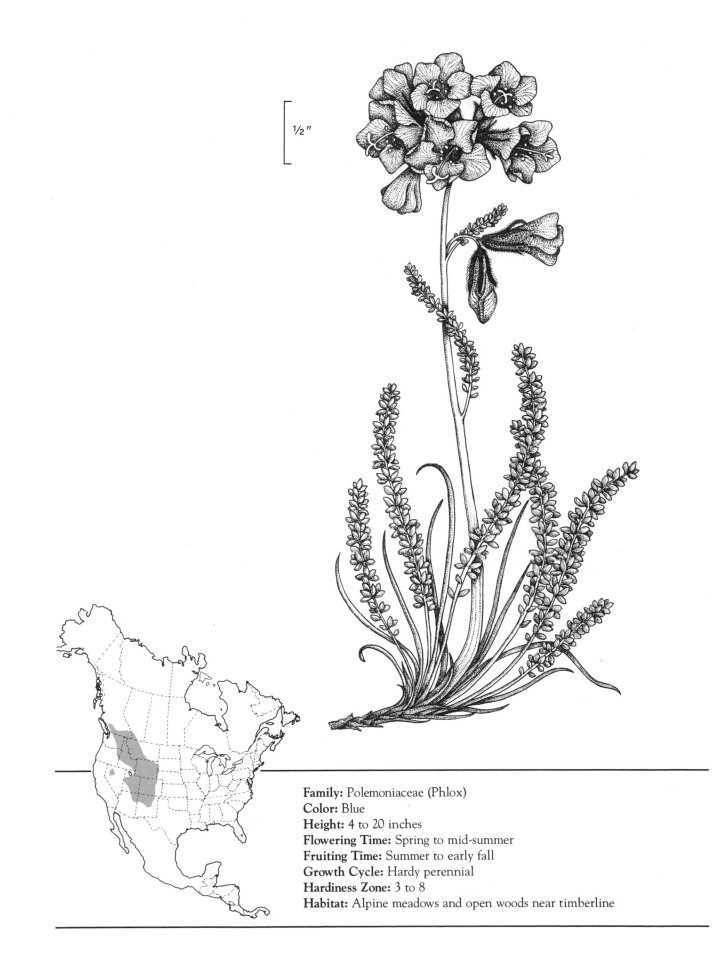

½"

Family: Polemoniaceae (Phlox)
Color: Blue
Height: 4 to 20 inches
Flowering Time: Spring to mid-summer
Fruiting Time: Summer to early fall
Growth Cycle: Hardy perennial
Hardiness Zone: 3 to 8
Habitat: Alpine meadows and open woods near timberline

SKY PILOT (*Polemonium viscosum*)

FOOTHILL SPECIES

The cold winters and hot summers of the western mountain foothills between 5,500 and 8,000 feet may present difficulties for conventional gardens: the growing season is relatively short and soil moisture reserves are frequently depleted by mid-summer. Foothill wildflowers are adapted to survive in these conditions as are many of the species described in Southwestern and Midwestern editions of *The Wildflower Gardener's Guide*. **Rocky Mountain penstemon** (*Penstemon strictus*), **Oregon grape** (*Mahonia repens*), **blue flax** (*Linum lewisii*), **sulfur-flowered eriogonum** (*Eriogonum umbellatum*), and **bitterroot** (*Lewisia rediviva*), all of which are included in other sections of this book, can be grown at lower elevations if planted in gardens with some protection from hot dry summer winds.

Xeriscape! Water, an increasingly scarce resource, is perhaps *the* primary ingredient in foothill gardening. Water-conserving gardening practices, collectively called "xeriscaping," are becoming increasingly popular in much of the West, and are described in detail on pages 22–23. Foothill wildflowers can play a central role in creating water-efficient xeriscapes, but other species should be considered as well. **Butterfly weed** (*Asclepias tuberosa*) has striking clusters of bright orange crown-shaped flowers which, as its common name suggests, attract many species of butterflies. The flowers of the **desert mallow** (*Sphaeralcea coccinea*) are also orange, resembling small hollyhocks. **Prairie smoke** (*Geum triflorum*) has attractive clusters of 3 dusty red flowers that produce wispy, downy fruit heads rising above light blue-green foliage.

If you are planning a meadow, **California poppy** (*Eschscholzia californica*), with its large golden-orange flowers, mixed with the powder blue blossoms of **blue flax** and the rich yellows of **lance-leaved coreopsis** (*Coreopsis lanceolata*) and **black-eyed Susan** (*Rudbeckia hirta*), make a spectacular xeriscape.

Numerous native shrubs can also enhance the foothill garden. The 3–8-foot **Apache plume** (*Fallugia paradoxa*) has dense semi-evergreen foliage that turns coppery in the fall. Its single white roselike flower blooms in the spring and produces showy pink plumelike fruits by the summer. It should be planted in the full sun, can withstand considerable drought, and will help control ero-

Foothill garden.

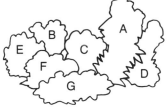

A. Rocky Mtn. beeplant
B. Blue flax
C. Blanketflower
D. Scarlet gilia
E. Mexican hat
F. Mule's ears
G. Tufted evening primrose

sion. **Sagebrush** (*Artemisia tridentata*) can grow even taller than Apache plume; its small, dense branches covered with ½-inch-long, hairy, gray, aromatic leaves can make an effective background screen. Smaller subspecies are also available if your space is limited. Another drought-resistant woody plant is **winterfat** (*Ceratoides lanata*), a low-growing shrub that tends to spread with age. Both the fruits and leaf surfaces of this 12–18-inch-high shrub are covered with wooly white hairs, making it glow in the sun.

Apart from the evergreen **ponderosa pine**, **juniper**, and **pinon pine** trees that dominate the foothill woodlands, **Gambel's oak** (*Quercus gambelii*) makes an excellent background or accent planting. It has deeply lobed, deciduous leaves and typically grows slowly up to 25 feet in height. **Rocky Mountain maple** (*Acer glabrum*), another small deciduous tree species, is effective in the foothill garden. Its broad green leaves, borne on wine-red twigs, turn yellow or even red in the fall.

ROCKY MOUNTAIN BEEPLANT
Cleome serrulata

(Beeplant, pink cleome, *cleome dente*)

This annual of the Great Plains and foothills of the Rockies looks like a softer version of the garden spider-flower (*Cleome spinosa*). The smooth, 1½–4-foot stems are sometimes branched near the top, creating a spreading crown up to 3 feet wide. Rocky Mountain beeplant has compound leaves consisting of 3 leaflets joined at the base. The edges of the smooth, dark green, lance-shaped, 1–3-inch-long leaflets frequently have a few minute teeth, giving this plant the Latin name *serrulata*, meaning "somewhat saw-toothed." The lower leaves have long petioles, while the leaves near the top of the plant are attached directly to the stem. The attractive flowers have 4 clawed ½-inch-long petals of white, pink, or lavender. Numerous long white or pink stamens project beyond the petals and the 4 sepals, which are united at their bases. In the center of the flower the ovary sits atop a long stalk with a gland at its base. This gland produces copious amounts of nectar attracting a wide variety of insects, especially bees, and, as its common name suggests, this wildflower is frequently cultivated as a nectar source in honey production. Pollen can fertilize ovules of the same plant, but the seeds so produced are not as likely to germinate as the products of cross-pollination. The flowering season lasts from early summer to the first frost. The flowers near the bottom of the cylindrical cluster open first, and as flowering progresses and the long ½-inch fruit pods develop the cluster starts to elongate. The rounded brown corn-shaped seeds with a prominently curved groove fall out of the ruptured pod at maturity. Rocky Mountain beeplant accumulates nitrogen from the soil, sometimes to levels toxic to livestock. Its leaves also produce glucosinolates, compounds related to mustard oil, which help the leaves and seeds resist damage from insects. More of these compounds are produced by plants growing in open, dry soils than by those growing in moist, shady soils, which may explain why the plant survives better and produces more seeds in dry areas. Despite these compounds, the leaves are esteemed by the caterpillars of checkered white (*Pontia protodice*) and western white (*P. occidentalis*) butterflies. Native Americans used the foliage for food, to make a black dye, and to treat stomach disorders and fever. The seeds are edible, but not widely sought after, except by birds and pocket mice.

CULTURE: Rocky Mountain beeplant is easy to grow on dry sandy soils in the full sun.

PROPAGATION: Like other annuals, this one can be grown only from seed. No seed treatment is necessary, but moist stratification (90 days at 4°C) appears to enhance germination, as do light and nitrate fertilizer enrichment. Plant the seeds in the fall or early spring, ⅓ inch deep in the desired location. Keep seeds and seedlings moist until established and then keep on the dry side. On well-drained sites it will self-seed prolifically.

COMPANIONS: Blanketflower, tufted evening primrose, Mexican hat.

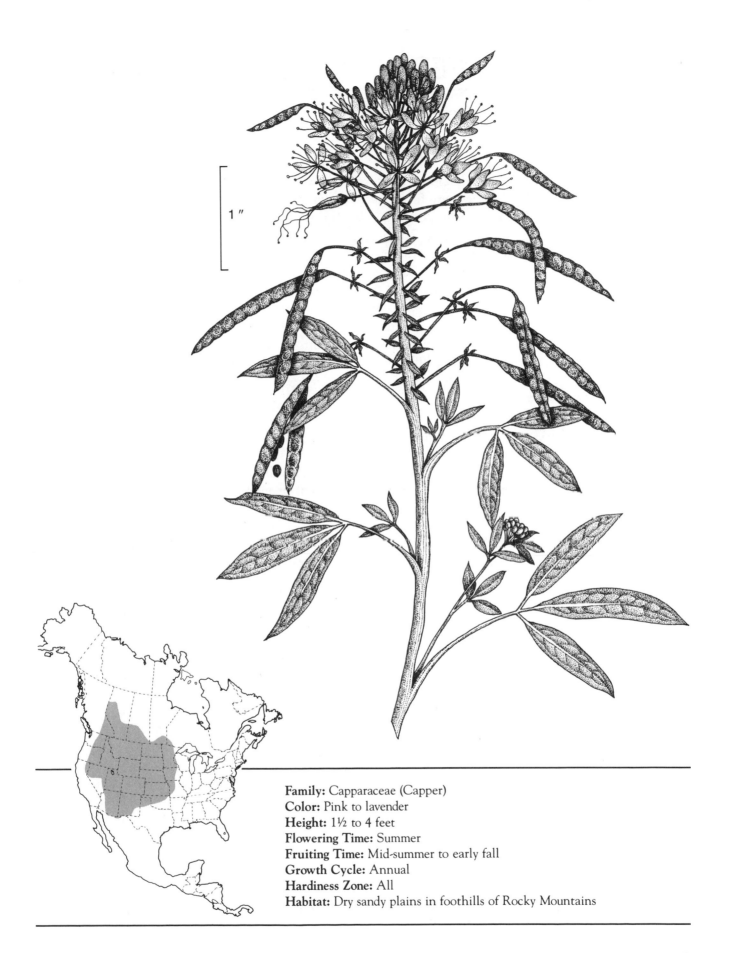

1 "

Family: Capparaceae (Capper)
Color: Pink to lavender
Height: 1½ to 4 feet
Flowering Time: Summer
Fruiting Time: Mid-summer to early fall
Growth Cycle: Annual
Hardiness Zone: All
Habitat: Dry sandy plains in foothills of Rocky Mountains

ROCKY MOUNTAIN BEEPLANT (*Cleome serrulata*)

BLANKETFLOWER

Gaillardia aristata

(Indian blanket, gaillardia, *gaillarde*)

This half-hardy perennial blankets parts of the dry Rocky Mountain foothills and northern Great Plains with yellow and red daisylike flowers all summer long. Blanketflower was first collected by the Lewis and Clark expedition in 1806 and within a decade was offered in European seed catalogs. The large garden blanketflower most often sold by nurseries, however, is the hybrid *Gaillardia* x *grandiflora*, the product of a series of crosses between G. *aristata* and its annual relative G. *pulchella*. Blanketflower's thick, hairy, dandelionlike leaves clasp the slender hairy stems of this erect, 2–4-foot plant. The inch-long ray flowers have yellow, 3-toothed tips and dark red to purple bases. While in the bud, the disc flowers are frequently red-orange, but as the fuzzy, 5-lobed flowers open they are generally the same color as the bases of the ray flowers. Tufts of hairs project from the tops of the 1/8-inch, conical, seedlike fruits. The plant's fuzzy hairs can cause a skin rash in people with sensitive skin.

CULTURE:
Blanketflower is adaptable to most sunny locations and is not particular about soils if they are well drained. It grows best in soils with slight to moderate acidity (pH 5.0-6.5), but will even tolerate alkaline conditions with soil pH of 8.0. Don't bother adding compost or other soil amendments to areas contemplated for blanketflower; it does best in infertile soils. While it is extremely hardy (to hardiness zone 3) when grown in its native dry range, it is only half-hardy in humid regions of the Northwest and should be mulched heavily for the winter. Once established, blanketflower is quite drought resistant. It is an excellent choice for meadows and xeriscaping in the foothills of the Rockies or as a cut flower anywhere. The flowering season can be prolonged by removing withering flowers before they set seed.

PROPAGATION:
Blanketflower can easily be propagated by seed or root division, and softwood stem cuttings are also possible. No chilling treatment of the seed is needed; simply plant in the fall or spring 1/8-¼ inch deep in a sunny location on well-drained soil. The seeds may also be started indoors in the early spring and transplanted to permanent locations after all danger of frost has passed. Germination takes only a week or two and plants may flower by the end of the first summer. Make root divisions in the early spring. Divide the taproot vertically, being sure each section has at least one bud and as many smaller lateral roots as possible. Plant sections 10-12 inches apart with the buds just at the soil surface. Since blanketflower is not a long-lived perennial, it may be necessary to divide the clumps every 2 or 3 years to keep it growing vigorously. Softwood cuttings can be made from the stems in the late spring, but seed or root division propagation is easier.

COMPANIONS:
Mexican hat, blue flax, scarlet gilia, Rocky Mountain beeplant, mule's ears.

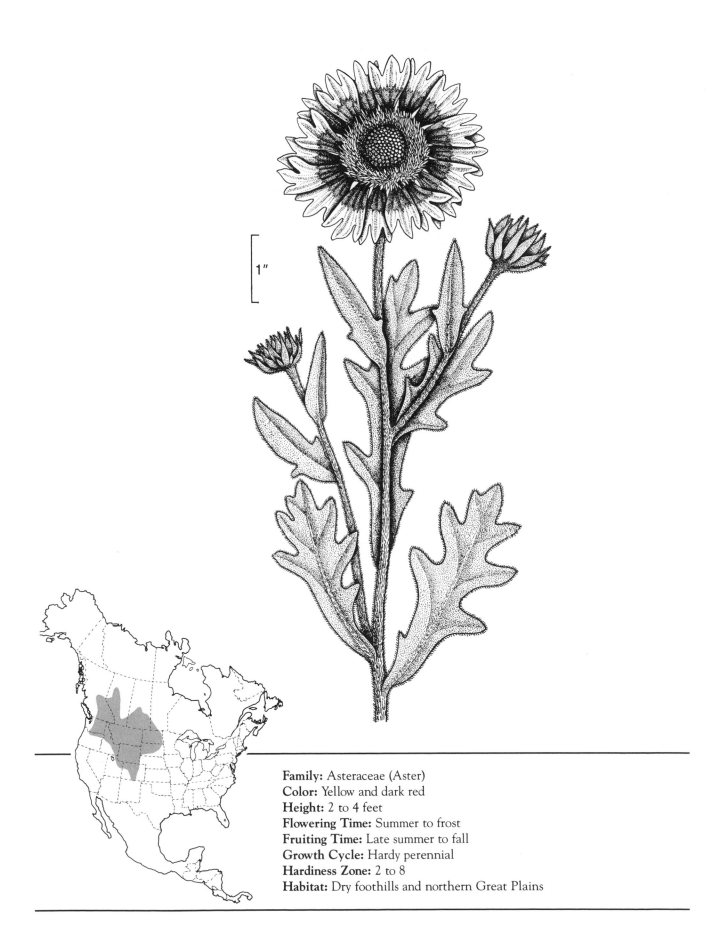

Family: Asteraceae (Aster)
Color: Yellow and dark red
Height: 2 to 4 feet
Flowering Time: Summer to frost
Fruiting Time: Late summer to fall
Growth Cycle: Hardy perennial
Hardiness Zone: 2 to 8
Habitat: Dry foothills and northern Great Plains

BLANKETFLOWER *(Gaillardia aristata)*

SCARLET GILIA

Ipomopsis aggregata
(Gilia aggregata)

(Skyrocket gilia, desert trumpets, skunk flower)

It is easy to guess why Captain Meriwether Lewis added this plant to the botanical collection of the Lewis and Clark expedition in northern Idaho in 1806: its dark ferny foliage and bright red trumpet-shaped flowers attract the attention of humans and hummingbirds alike. The 1–2-inch, curved, highly dissected leaves are dense near the bottom and sparse higher on the 1–2½-foot stems. Fine hairs covering the foliage cause rain water to bead up on the leaf surfaces, and emit a faintly skunky odor when the leaves are crushed. The 5 to 15 blossoms flower in no particular order on the stem, but new flowers usually open in the mid-afternoon. Most of the ¾–1½-inch-long flowers have 5 sepals, 5 petals, 5 stamens producing pollen varying in color from yellow to blue, a 3-chambered ovary, and 3 stigma lobes, but many plants have a different number of these features. The anthers shed their pollen the day the flower opens. They are positioned on the lower side of the corolla tube, so the rufous, calliope, and broad-tailed hummingbirds (and, less frequently, hawkmoths and bees) that visit the scentless flowers take pollen on the chin. The next day the style elongates past the anthers, and the 3 stigmatic surfaces open. Several hours after pollen is deposited on the stigma lobes they close together, preventing the deposit of additional pollen grains. The dozen small seeds in the oval capsule fruits mature about a month after pollination. Native Americans obtained blue dye by crushing the roots, glue by boiling down the whole plant, and laxatives and cures for venereal disease from the leaves. Recently several compounds with anti-cancer properties, such as schottenol glucoside and ipomopsin, have been found in scarlet gilia leaves.

CULTURE: Grow scarlet gilia in full sun on well-drained soil. Otherwise, it is not choosy about garden conditions such as soil pH, and can be grown in hardiness zones 8-4. Don't worry if some of the plants are eaten by mule deer and elk, since browsing prior to the flowering season stimulates growth of multiple flowering stems and increases flower production. If pocket gophers dig up and eat the entire plant, they may be controlled by burying hardware cloth, which the plant can grow through, just under the soil surface.

PROPAGATION: Scarlet gilia reproduces only by seed. No seed treatment is necessary; just scratch the seeds into the surface of the soil and keep moist until the seedlings are established. The first year the plant is a nestlike basal rosette, 4 inches in diameter. Flowering occurs any time from 1 to 8 years later.

COMPANIONS: Blue flax, sulfur-flowered eriogonum, tufted evening primrose, blanketflower, Rocky Mountain penstemon.

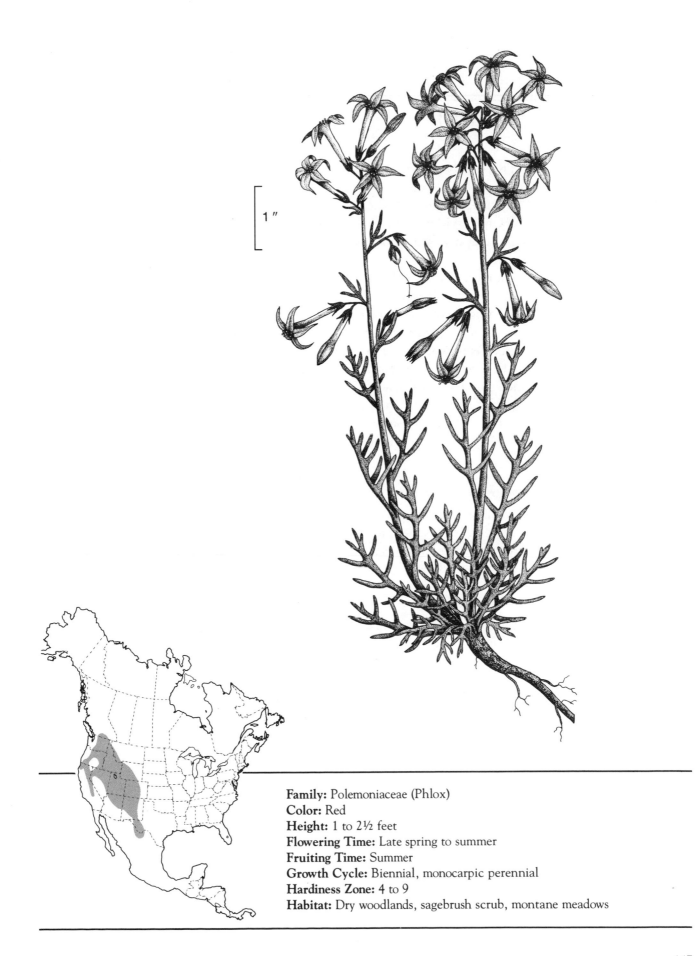

Family: Polemoniaceae (Phlox)
Color: Red
Height: 1 to 2½ feet
Flowering Time: Late spring to summer
Fruiting Time: Summer
Growth Cycle: Biennial, monocarpic perennial
Hardiness Zone: 4 to 9
Habitat: Dry woodlands, sagebrush scrub, montane meadows

SCARLET GILIA *(Ipomopsis aggregata)*

BLUE FLAX

Linum lewisii
(*Linum perenne* ssp. *lewisii*)

(Prairie flax, *lin de Lewis*)

This widely distributed perennial of the western two-thirds of North America is considered by some to be a subspecies of the European plant from which linen is made. Like several other wildflowers in this book, the species is named in honor of Captain Meriwether Lewis of the Lewis and Clark expedition. Blue flax stands 1–3 feet high with clusters of 1½-inch sky blue flowers arching to one side atop slender stems. Flowering begins with the long days of spring and continues through summer. The 5-petaled flowers usually last only a day before withering in the hot sun, but new flowers appear in the cluster every day. At the center of the flower are 5 light-colored stamens and 5 stigmas. The fruit is a ¼-inch capsule containing 10 shiny, dark, flattened 1/8-inch seeds that are gummy when wet. The several stems, which arise in a clump, are densely covered by narrow, 1-inch leaves. These contain *linamarin*, a glycoside compound that can produce low levels of cyanide and may cause livestock poisoning, although the inch-long, white, red, and black caterpillars of the variegated fritillary butterfly (*Euptoieta claudia*) eat them with no ill effects. Native Americans concocted a medicine for sore eyes from the roots of the plant and used the stems for stomach disorders.

CULTURE: Blue flax is a plant of open habitats and thus requires full sun. It will grow robustly on soils ranging from alkaline to acidic (pH 5.0-7.5) as long as the soil is well drained and dry. It grows well in gardens, but should not be watered excessively. A very hardy perennial, blue flax can be grown in hardiness zones 2-10. This drought-tolerant wildflower is excellent for meadows and xeriscaping.

PROPAGATION: Blue flax is usually propagated by seed. Root division is generally not as successful since the plant is difficult to transplant. In the fall, plant the seeds 1/8 inch deep in the desired location. Though seeds can be planted in the spring, seedling establishment is far better after fall planting. While the germination of the seeds of European flax (*L. perenne*) requires light, those of blue flax do not and germinate rather rapidly in spring as soil temperatures rise toward 70°F. Blue flax will generally flower the first year and will self-seed once established.

COMPANIONS: Blanketflower, Mexican hat, mule's ears.

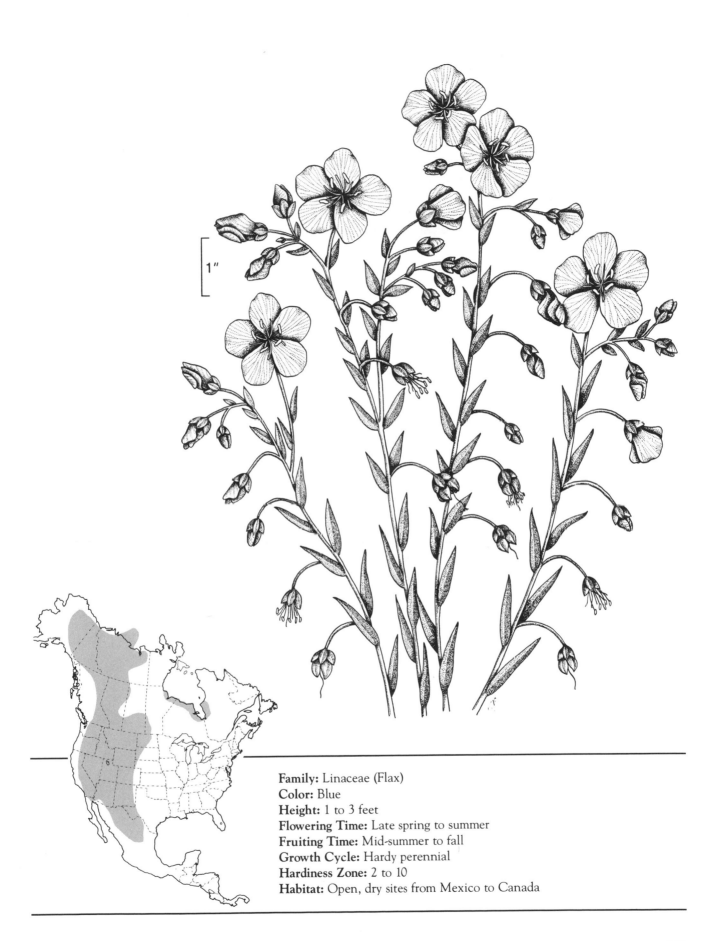

Family: Linaceae (Flax)
Color: Blue
Height: 1 to 3 feet
Flowering Time: Late spring to summer
Fruiting Time: Mid-summer to fall
Growth Cycle: Hardy perennial
Hardiness Zone: 2 to 10
Habitat: Open, dry sites from Mexico to Canada

BLUE FLAX *(Linium lewisii)*

TUFTED EVENING PRIMROSE *Oenothera caespitosa*

(White evening primrose, stemless evening primrose)

The leaves of this foothill perennial grow in "tufted" rosettes an inch or two above the ground, giving it both its common name and the Latin name *caespitosa*. Its attractive blue-green, lance-shaped, 3–8-inch-long leaves are covered with fine, silky hairs, and have wavy or slightly toothed margins and winged petioles. Several varieties of tufted evening primrose, on various western mountain ranges, are distinguished by the amount and distribution of hairs on the leaves. Flowering begins in mid-spring in California and continues to mid-summer in the high elevations in the Rockies, with several 6–12-inch shoots bearing single reddish buds emerging from the center of the leafy rosette. While *O. caespitosa* is not related to the true primroses, the name evening primrose is well applied since its fragrant white flowers open at night, are pollinated by hawkmoths, and turn pink by noon the next day. The showy flowers have 4 broadly heart-shaped petals and 8 stamens that sit atop a very long, inferior, 4-part ovary. The ovary is surrounded by a slender calyx tube, topped by 4 sepals and a long thin style that ends in a cross-shaped stigma. Tufted evening primrose fruits resemble warty, 1–2-inch-long pickles when young, but become tan and woody when mature during the summer and fall. The rough, dark brown, furrowed, 1/10-inch seeds are eaten by ground birds such as mourning doves and quail. The thick woody roots sometimes produce additional small rosettes from the rootcrown branches. Native Americans pounded the roots, making a paste to apply to sores and to reduce inflammation.

CULTURE: Tufted evening primrose grows best on gravelly, shalely, sandy soils with good drainage. Dry soil is a must, especially during the winter, since cold wet soils will tend to rot roots. The long flowering season of this wildflower can be further prolonged with a bit of extra moisture if the summer is especially dry. Tufted evening primrose is an excellent choice for beds and borders.

PROPAGATION: Propagate tufted evening primrose from seed, because its long woody roots are difficult to divide. No seed treatment is necessary, but germination is best in the dark and at relatively cool (60-70° F) temperatures. Plant the seeds ¼ inch deep in the fall in the desired locations. Keep the seedlings moist, but not wet, until they are established.

COMPANIONS: Mule's ears, Rocky Mountain beeplant, blanketflower.

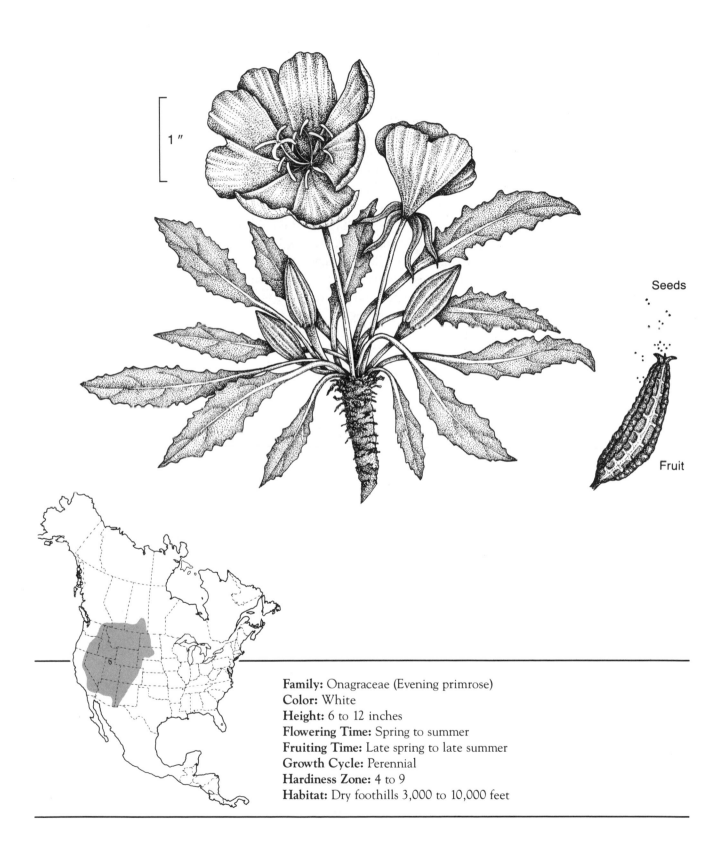

1 "

Seeds

Fruit

Family: Onagraceae (Evening primrose)
Color: White
Height: 6 to 12 inches
Flowering Time: Spring to summer
Fruiting Time: Late spring to late summer
Growth Cycle: Perennial
Hardiness Zone: 4 to 9
Habitat: Dry foothills 3,000 to 10,000 feet

TUFTED EVENING PRIMROSE *(Oenothera caespitosa)*

MEXICAN HAT

Ratibida columnifera
(R. columnaris, Lepachys columnaris)

(Red Mexican hat, upright coneflower, prairie coneflower)

The central brown discs of this member of the aster family protrude ½–2½ inches beyond the drooping ray flowers, making the 1–3-inch flower heads resemble sombreros. As the dark purple tubular flowers start blooming from the bases of the discs, the hats even appear to have hatbands. This hardy perennial has branched, 1½–3-foot-high shoots with feathery, deeply cleft leaves on the lower portion of the stem, frequently with short, stiff bristles. Flowering begins in the long days of late spring and continues until fall. The 3 to 7 flowers are borne on leafless stems, making the Mexican hat an excellent cut flower. Ray flowers may be entirely yellow or yellow with red bases, the latter form often called red Mexican hat. Dakota skipper butterflies (*Hesperia dacotae*) use Mexican hat as a nectar source even though it conceals camouflaged predators such as ambush bugs (*Phymata*) and flower spiders (*Misumena vatia*). The flower spider is white or yellow but can change its color to fit the color scheme of the flower it hides upon. The seedlike 1/8-inch fruit has fringe on one edge and two teeth projecting from one end. The root system is a diffuse taproot. Although confusion can arise from the many common names associated with the two different color forms of Mexican hat and the frequent listing of the plant as *Ratibida columnaris* or *Lepachys columnaris* in seed catalogs, they are all one species.

CULTURE: Grow Mexican hat in full sun on well-drained soils. It prefers soils that are slightly acidic to alkaline (pH 6-8), but is adaptable to normal garden conditions. Once established, this superb meadow plant requires little water, being quite drought tolerant, and can withstand competition from other wildflowers and grasses.

PROPAGATION: This is one of the easiest wildflowers to propagate from seed, either in the desired location or in flats for future transplanting. In the fall or spring plant the seeds ¼ inch deep in sandy loam or sandy soil. Unstratified seeds will germinate, but the best results are obtained if seeds are chilled at 40°F for 9 weeks, then germinated at 80°F. Germination is rapid once temperatures are warm. Seedlings need moisture while becoming established. Mexican hat can be grown as an annual if the growing season is long enough. In cold climates, start seedlings indoors in late winter and transplant 8-12 inches apart in the spring. Plants from seed usually bloom the second year. In hardiness zone 5 and colder regions, give Mexican hat a good overwinter mulch, and remove it in the spring.

COMPANIONS: Blanketflower, blue flax, and many others.

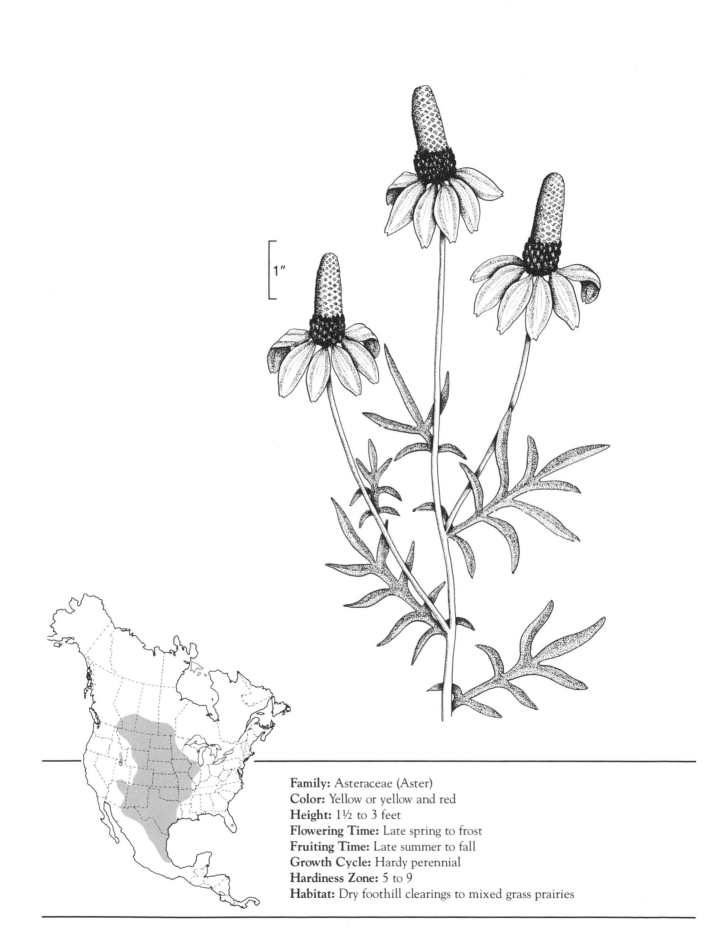

Family: Asteraceae (Aster)
Color: Yellow or yellow and red
Height: 1½ to 3 feet
Flowering Time: Late spring to frost
Fruiting Time: Late summer to fall
Growth Cycle: Hardy perennial
Hardiness Zone: 5 to 9
Habitat: Dry foothill clearings to mixed grass prairies

MEXICAN HAT (*Ratibida columnifera*)

MULE'S EARS

Wyethia amplexicaulis

(Mule's-ear wyethia, dwarf sunflower)

The long leaves of this member of the aster family, which grows among the sagebrush in foothills between the Sierra Nevada and Rocky Mountains, resemble the ears of a mule; rather than being hairy, however, the leaves are covered with a resinous varnish. From amid clumps of dark green, aromatic, 8–24-inch foliage rise 1–2-foot-high stems, bearing clasping leaves and a cluster of several 3–5-inch-wide sunflowerlike blossoms. The centermost flower head in the cluster tends to be the largest. The 13 to 21 1–1½-inch ray flowers are bright yellow and the numerous disc flowers, a deeper yellow. The 4-sided seedlike fruit of mule's ears has a low crown of scales at one end. Thick taproots and fibrous roots extend from the underground rhizome. The rhizome's overwintering buds, covered with bud scales, resemble buds found on woody shrubs and trees. On western rangelands, sheep graze upon mule's ears only after more desired species are consumed and then prefer the flowers to the coarse leaves. It is obvious why this plant is sometimes called dwarf sunflower; the other name, wyethia, is in honor of Captain Nathaniel J. Wyeth, who led the botanical expedition that discovered this genus in the 1830s.

CULTURE: Mule's ears, while a plant of open situations, should be given ample moisture during the flowering season. Moist but well-drained, clayey loams are ideal for this hardy perennial. It grows best where the soil pH is close to neutral (pH 6.0-7.5). Mule's ears start growing in March, peak in vigor by mid-spring, and then typically dry up by mid-July. Because of this seasonal growth pattern it should not be used by itself for erosion control, but should be interplanted with other species to provide a more continuous cover. Mule's ears populations benefit from periodic light burning.

PROPAGATION: The easiest way to propagate mule's ears is by the only way it occurs in the field: from seed. Seed should be planted ¼ inch deep in the fall in permanent locations or in deep flats that are left out for the winter. Seeds should receive a moist stratification treatment (at least 1 month at 40°F) for proper germination to occur in the spring. If flats or pots are used, transplant the dormant plants to permanent locations during the next fall. Mule's ears can also be propagated by rhizome division. Divide the rhizome in the fall or early spring, each piece having at least one bud. Plant the divisions 8-12 inches apart with the bud just below the soil surface.

COMPANIONS: Blue flax, Mexican hat, blanketflower, tufted evening primrose.

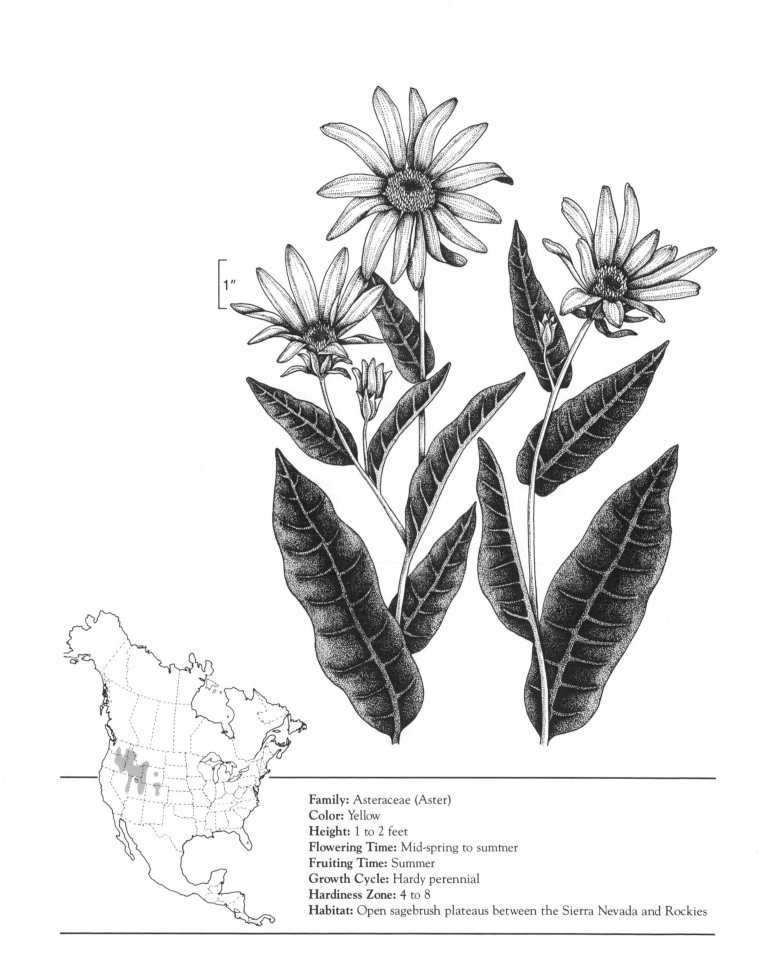

Family: Asteraceae (Aster)
Color: Yellow
Height: 1 to 2 feet
Flowering Time: Mid-spring to summer
Fruiting Time: Summer
Growth Cycle: Hardy perennial
Hardiness Zone: 4 to 8
Habitat: Open sagebrush plateaus between the Sierra Nevada and Rockies

MULE'S EARS *(Wyethia amplexicaulis)*

Appendixes

Suppliers

British Columbia

Alpenflora Gardens
17985 40th Avenue
Surrey, BC V3S 4N8
Sells live plants, retail and wholesale, by mail. Catalogs $2.50 and $5.00, refundable with purchase. Specializes in alpines and rock garden plants.

California

C.H. Baccus
900 Boynton Avenue
San Jose, CA 95117

Sells home-grown live plants by mail order. For free list, enclose a self-addressed, stamped legal-size envelope.

Berkeley Horticultural Nursery
1310 McGee Avenue
Berkeley, CA 94703-1098
(415)526-4704

Sells seeds, live plants, and books over the counter. Specializes in California native plants.

California Flora Nursery
Somers & D Streets
P.O. Box 3
Fulton, CA 95439
(707)528-8813

Sells live plants, retail and wholesale, over the counter. Free availability list. Specializes in California natives.

J.L. Hudson, Seedsman
P.O. Box 1058
Redwood City, CA 94064

Sells seeds and books, retail and wholesale, by mail. Catalog $1.00. Many species of wildflowers, shrubs, and trees.

The Natural Gardening Company
217 San Anselmo Avenue
San Anselmo, CA 94960

Sells seeds, books, and environmentally sound gardening supplies, by mail and over the counter. Free catalog. Seeds available in bulk.

Moon Mountain Wildflowers
P.O. Box 34
Morro Bay, CA 93443

Sells seeds and books, retail and wholesale, by mail order, phone order, and over the counter. Catalog $2.00. Specializes in N. American native wildflower seeds, in packets and bulk.

Pacific Tree Farms
4301 Lynwood Drive
Chula Vista, CA 92010
(619)422-2400

Sells live plants and books, retail and wholesale, over the counter, by phone, and mail order. Catalog $2.00. Specializes in hard-to-find trees and plants.

Las Pilitas Nursery
Star Route Box 23X
Las Pilitas Road
Santa Margarita, CA 93453
(805)438-5992

Sells seeds and live plants, retail and wholesale, over the counter Saturdays only and by mail. Catalog $4.00. Specializes in California native plants.

Redwood City Seed Company
P.O. Box 361
Redwood City, CA 94064
(415)325-7333

Sells seeds, books, and bunchgrass plants, retail and wholesale, by phone and mail order. Catalog $1.00. Specializes in California native wildflowers and grasses.

Clyde Robin Seed Company
P.O. Box 2366
Castro Valley, CA 94546
(415)785-0425

Sells seeds and books, retail and wholesale, by mail, phone order, and over the counter. Free catalog. Full range of wildflower seeds.

Wildflowers International, Inc.
P.O. Box 131
Elk, CA 95432
(707)877-3400

Sells seeds wholesale only, by phone. Brochure describes custom mixture design services.

Yerba Buena Nursery
19500 Skyline Boulevard
Woodside, CA 94062
(415)851-1668

Sells seeds and live plants, over the counter and occasionally by mail order. For free catalog enclose 2-oz. postage stamped, self-addressed legal-size envelope. Specializes in California native wildflowers, shrubs, and trees.

Colorado

Applewood Seed Company
5380 Vivian Street
Arvada, CO 80002
(303)431-6283

Sells seeds, retail and wholesale, by mail and phone order. Specializes in wildflower, herb, and specialty seeds.

Old Farm Nursery
5550 Indiana Street
Golden, CO 80403
(800)635-5083
(303)278-0754

Sells live plants, retail and wholesale, by phone, mail order, and over the counter. Free catalog. Specializes in rock garden and alpine widlflowers.

Dean Swift Seed Company
P.O. Box B
Jaroso, CO 81138-0028
(719)672-3739

Sells seeds, wholesale, by mail and phone order. Free catalog. Specializes in native wildflowers, grasses, shrubs, and conifers.

Idaho

High Altitude Gardens
P.O. Box 4619
500 Bell Drive # 7
Ketchum, ID 83340
(800)874-7333

Sells seeds and live plants, retail and wholesale, by phone and mail order.

Catalog $2.00. Specializes in wildflowers and native grasses for harsh montane climates.

Northplan/Mountain Seed
P.O. Box 9107
Moscow, ID 83843-1607
(208)882-8040
FAX (208)882-7446

Sells seeds and live plants, by mail and phone order. For free seed list, enclose a self-addressed, stamped, legal-size envelope.

Solar Green, Ltd.
Route 1
Box 115 A
Moore, ID 83255
(208)554-2821

Sells seeds by mail order. Catalog $1.50. Specializes in alpine wildflowers, especially Idaho.

Winterfeld Ranch Seed Company
P.O. Box 97
Swan Valley, ID 83449
(208)483-3683

Sells seeds wholesale, by phone and mail order. Catalog available.

Montana

Lawyer Nursery, Inc.
950 Highway 200 West
Plains, MT 59859
(406)826-3881
FAX (406)826-5700

Sells seeds and live woody plant seedlings, wholesale, by phone and mail order. Free catalog.

New Jersey

Thompson & Morgan
P.O. Box 1308
Jackson, NJ 08527-0308
(201)363-2225
FAX (201)363-9356

Sells seeds, wholesale and retail, by phone and mail order. Free catalog.

New Mexico

Curtis & Curtis
Star Route Box 8A
Clovis, NM 88101
(505)762-4759

Sells seeds, wholesale and retail, over the counter and by phone. Specializes in native grasses.

C.H. & E. Diebold, Ltd.
268 La Ladera Road
Los Lunas, NM 87031

Sells seeds wholesale. Specializes in western wildflowers.

New Mexico Native Plant Nursery
907 Pope Street
Silver City, NM 88061
(505)538-5201

Sells seeds of woody plants native to New Mexico, retail and wholesale, over the counter, by phone, and mail order. Price list available.

Plants of the Southwest
930 Baca Street Santa Fe, NM 87501
(505)983-1548

Sells seeds, live plants, and books, wholesale and retail, over the counter, by phone, and mail order. Catalog $2.00. Specializes in grasses, wildflowers, shrubs, vegetables, and biological controls for the West.

Oregon

Callahan Seeds
6045 Foley Road
Central Point, OR 97502
(503)855-1164

Sells seeds, wholesale and retail, by phone and mail order. For catalog enclose a stamped, self-addressed, legal-size envelope. Specializes in western woody plants and wildflowers.

Forestfarm
990 Tetherow Road
Williams, OR 97544-9599

Sells live plants by mail order. Catalog $2.00. Specializes in nursery-grown, containerized native plants.

Goodwin Creek Gardens
P.O. Box 83
Williams, OR 97544
(503)846-7357

Sells seeds and live plants, over the counter, by phone, and mail order. Catalog $1.00, refunded with purchase. Specializes in herbs and native wildflowers.

Russell & Yvonne Graham
4030 Eagle Crest Road, N.W.
Salem, OR 97304

Sells live plants, wholesale and retail, by mail order. Catalog $2.00, refunded with purchase. Specializes in hardy native wildflowers and ferns.

Great Western Seed Company
P.O. Box 387
Albany, OR 97321
(800)547-4063

Sells seeds wholesale, by phone.

Nature's Garden
Route 1, Box 488
Beaverton, OR 97007

Sells live plants and seeds, by mail order. Catalog $1.25, refunded with purchase.

Specializes in alpines, ferns, and western wildflowers.

Nichols Garden Nursery
1190 North Pacific Highway
Albany, OR 97321
(503)928-9280

Sells seeds and books, retail, by phone and mail order. Free catalog.

Siskiyou Rare Plant Nursery
2825 Cummings Road
Medford, OR 97501
(503)772-6846

Sells live plants and books, over the counter, by phone, and mail order. Catalog $2.00, refunded with purchase. Specializes in hardy native alpine, rock garden, and woodland plants.

Pennsylvania

W. Atlee Burpee & Company
300 Park Avenue
Warminster, PA 18991-0003
(800)888-1447

Sells seeds, live plants, and books, retail and wholesale, by phone and mail order. Free catalog. Specializes in a wide variety of plant seeds and gardening aids.

Utah

Granite Seed Company
P.O. Box 177
Lehi, UT 84043
(801)531-1456

Sells seeds wholesale, by phone and mail order. Catalog $3.00. Specializes in western wildflowers, grasses, and shrubs for erosion control.

Washington

Abundant Life Seed Foundation
1029 Lawrence P.O. Box 772
Port Townsend, WA 98368
(206)385-7192

Sells seeds and books, retail and wholesale, over the counter, by phone, and mail order. Catalog $1.00. Specializes in Pacific Northwest native plant seeds.

Skyline Nursery
464-13 Heath Road
Sequim, WA 98382
(206)683-2294

Sells live plants, retail and wholesale, by mail order. Catalog $1.00. Specialize in western alpines, grasses, and hardy native perennials.

Frosty Hollow
Box 53
Langley, WA 98260
(206)221-2332

Sells seeds, wholesale and retail, by mail order. Seed list available, $1.00. Specializes in northwestern wildflower, shrub, and tree seeds.

Botanical Gardens

Alberta

Devonian Botanic Garden
University of Alberta
Edmonton, Alberta T6G 2E1
(403)987-3054

Free. Open May–Sept 10 am–7 pm. Sells seeds to members, sells books. Collection of labeled native plants.

Arizona

The Arboretum at Flagstaff
P.O. Box 670
Flagstaff, AZ 86002
(602)774-1441

Free. Open all year 10 am–3 pm Monday–Friday. Guided tours and seminars on wildflower gardening.

British Columbia

University of British Columbia
  Botanical Garden
6501 NW Marine Drive
Vancouver, BC V6T 1W5
(604)228-3928

Entrance fee: $3.00 (free in winter). Open 10 am–dusk, daily. Sells seeds, live plants, and books. Special native and alpine gardens.

Van Dusen Gardens
5251 Oak Street
Vancouver, BC V6M 4H1
(604)266-7194

Entrance fee: $4.00 ($2.00 child). Open all year, except Christmas, 9 am–9 pm (summer), 10 am–4 pm (winter). Sells books, has seed exchange. Guided tours, special indoor exhibits.

California

Mendocino Coast Botanical Gardens
18220 N. Highway One
P.O. Box 1143
Fort Bragg, CA 95437
(707)964-4352

Entrance fee: $5.00. Open daily 9 am–5 pm (summer), 10 am–2 pm (winter). Sells live plants and books. Interpretive displays and trails through wild and cultivated plants.

Muir Woods National Monument
Mill Valley, CA 94941
(415)388-2595

Free. Open every day 8 am–sunset. Sells wildflower seeds and books. Ranger-led programs on redwood ecology.

Regional Parks Botanic Garden
Tilden Regional Park
Berkeley, CA 94708-1199
(415)841-8732

Free. Open all year 10 am–5 pm. Sells seeds, live plants, and books. Tours and lectures. Extensive collection of California native plants.

Strybing Arboretum &
  Botanical Gardens
Golden Gate Park
9th Ave. & Lincoln Way
San Francisco, CA 94122
(415)558-3622

Free. Open 8 am–4:30 pm weekdays, 10 am–5 pm weekends and holidays. Sells seeds, live plants, books. Theme walks and workshops on native plants. Tours.

University of California
  Botanical Garden
Centennial Drive
Berkeley, CA 94720
(415)642-3343

Free. Open every day but Christmas, 8:45 am–4:45 pm. Sells live plants and books. Lectures and field trips.

Colorado

Denver Botanic Gardens
1005 York Street
Denver, CO 80206
(303)331-4000

Entrance fee: $4.00 winter, $3.00 summer. Open daily 9:00 am–4:45 pm. Sells seeds, books, and has plant sale. Classes in native plant identification and use in landscaping. Large collection of western native plants.

Montana

Native Plant Gardens
University of Montana
University & Arthur Avenues
Missoula, MT 59801

Free. Open daylight hours. Native plant collection on campus of University of Montana.

Oregon

Berry Botanic Garden
11505 SW Summerville Avenue
Portland, OR 97219
(503)636-4112

Entrance fee: $2.00 donation. Open all year 8:00 am–5:00 pm Monday-Saturday. Wildflower walks and classes. Programs and speakers. Several plant sales.

Castle Crest Wildflower Gardens
Crater Lake National Park
Crater Lake, OR 97604

Entrance fee: admission to Crater Lake National Park. Open July–September, daylight hours.

Claire Hanley Arboretum
569 Hanley Road
Medford, OR 97501
(503)772-5110

Free. Open all year 8:00 am–4:30 pm Monday–Friday. Part of Oregon State University and a state Agricultural Experiment Station. Tours of various gardens.

Hoyt Arboretum
4000 SW Fairview Boulevard
Portland, OR 97221
(503)228-8732

Free. Open all year, daylight hours. Wildflower meadows and woodland trails with native plants.

Leach Botanical Garden
6704 SE 122nd Avenue
Portland, OR 97236
(503)761-9503

Free. Open all year, 10:00 am–4:00 pm (Tuesday–Saturday), 12:00 noon–4:00 pm (Sunday). Sells seeds, live plants, and books. Guided tours and lectures.

Mount Pisgah Arboretum
P.O. Box 5621
Eugene, OR 97405
(503)747-3817

Free. Open daily, all year. Sells seeds, live plants, and books. Nature walks and spring wildflower show.

Utah

Utah State University/
  Utah Botanical Gardens
1817 N. Main Street
Framington, UT 84025

Free. Open daily, all year. Sells books about native plants. Tours of gardens available.

Red Butte Gardens and Arboretum
Building 436, University of Utah
Salt Lake City, UT 84112
(801)581-5322

Open every day but Christmas, 9 am—sunset. Sells seeds, live plants, and books. Slide library.

Washington

John A. Finch Arboretum
West 3404 Woodland Boulevard
Spokane, WA 99204
(509)456-4381

Free. Open daily, all year. Trails with labeled native plants.

Northwest Native Garden
Point Defiance Park
5402 N. Shirley
Tacoma, WA 98407
(206)591-5328

Free. Open all year, daylight hours. Six botanic zones, maintained by the Tacoma Garden Club.

Sehome Hill Arboretum
Western Washington University
Bellingham, WA 98225
(206)676-6985

Free. Open daily, all year. Public tours, extensive trails through natural area.

Washington Park Arboretum
2300 Arboretum Drive E.
Seattle, WA 98112

mailing address:
University of Washington, XD-10
Seattle, WA 98195
(206)543-8800

Free. Open daily 7:00 am–dusk, visitor center open 10:00 am–4:00 pm weekdays, 12:00 noon–4:00 pm weekends. Sells books. Lectures and trips.

Native Plant and Horticultural Societies

British Columbia

Alpine Garden Club of
  British Columbia
Box 5161, MPO
Vancouver, BC V6B 4B2

Publishes Bulletin. *Seed exchanges and plant sales. Monthly meetings.*

California

California Native Plant Society
909 12th Street, Suite 116
Sacramento, CA 95814
(916)447-2677

Publishes Fremontia *and* CNPS Bulletin. *Twenty-eight chapters state-wide. Periodic plant sales, extensive publication list.*

California Non-Game Heritage
  Program
The Resource Agency
Department of Fish & Game
1416 9th Street, 12th Floor
Sacramento, CA 95814
(916)322-2493

Working to protect, restore, and manage California rare, threatened, and endangered plants. General information on California's endangered plants and programs to protect and manage their habitats.

Natural Reserve System
University of California
300 Lakeside Drive, 6th Floor
Oakland, CA 94612-3560
(415)987-0153

Publishes the NRS Transect. *Manages natural areas throughout California for teaching and research. Hosts open houses and tours.*

The Nature Conservancy
California Field Office
785 Market Street
San Francisco, CA 94130

Publishes the California Nature Conservancy Newsletter.

Colorado

Colorado Native Plant Society
Box 200
Fort Collins, CO 80522

Publishes a newsletter. Regional chapters. Sponsors field trips, seminars, and workshops.

Colorado Natural Areas Inventory
Department of Natural Resources
1313 Sherman Street, Room 718
Denver, CO 80203
(303)866-3311

State Natural Heritage Program Office.

The Nature Conservancy
Colorado Field Office
1244 Pine Street
Boulder, CO 80302
(303)444-2950

Upper Colorado Environmental
  Plant Center
P.O. Box 448
Meeker, CO 81641
(303)878-5003

Part of the network of plant material centers.

Idaho

Idaho Native Plant Society
(Pahove Chapter)
Box 9451
Boise, ID 83707

Idaho Natural Heritage Program
Department of Fish & Game
600 S. Walnut Street, Box 25
Boise, ID 83707
(208)334-3402

The Nature Conservancy
Idaho Field Office
P.O. Box 64
Sun Valley, ID 83353
(208)726-3007

Plant Materials Center
U.S.D.A. Soil Conservation Service
P.O. Box AA
Aberdeen, ID 83210

Part of the network of plant material centers.

Montana

Montana Native Plant Society
P.O. Box 992
Bozeman, MT 59771-0992

Publishes Kelseya. Various local chapters have monthly meetings. Field trips and programs on native flora.

Montana Natural Heritage Program
State Library Building
1515 East 6th Avenue
Helena, MT 59620
(406)444-3009

Ecological information on Montana's rare plants and animals.

The Nature Conservancy
Montana Field Office
P.O. Box 258
Helena, MT 59624
(406)443-0303

Publishes The Big Sky Field Office Newsletter.

New Mexico

Native Plant Society of New Mexico
P.O. Box 5917
Santa Fe, NM 87502

Publishes a newsletter. Sells books on native plants. Has source list for native plant suppliers. Five regional chapters.

The Nature Conservancy
New Mexico Field Office
107 Cienega Street
Santa Fe, NM 87501
(505)988-3867

New Mexico Natural Resources
    Survey Section
Villagra Building
Santa Fe, NM 87503
(505)827-7862

Plant Materials Center
U.S.D.A. Soil Conservation Service
1036 Miller Street SW Los Lunas,
NM 87031

Part of the network of plant material centers.

Oregon

Native Plant Society of Oregon
13285 S. Clackamas River Drive
Oregon City, OR 97045

Publishes Bulletin of NPSO. Monthly meetings of 10 chapters.

The Nature Conservancy
Oregon Field Office
1205 N.W. 25th Avenue
Portland, OR 97210
(503)228-9561

Utah

The Nature Conservancy
Great Basin Field Office
P.O. Box 11486, Pioneer Station
Salt Lake City, UT 84147-0486
(801)531-0999

Publishes TNC Great Basin Newsletter.

Utah Native Plant Society
c/o Utah State University/
Utah Botanical Gardens
1817 N. Main Street
Framington, UT 84025

Publishes The Sego Lily. Several regional chapters.

Washington

Operation Wildflower
Washington Chapter
State Federation of Garden Clubs
1416 170th Place NW
Bellevue, WA 98008
(206)747-0268

Sponsors annual wildflower workshops, encourages roadside planting of native plants.

The Nature Conservancy
Washington Field Office
1601 Second Avenue, Suite 910
Seattle, WA 98101
(206)728-9696

Washington Native Plant Society
c/o Dr. A.R. Kruckeberg
Department of Botany
University of Washington
Seattle, WA 98195

Washington Natural Heritage Program
Department of Natural Resources
Mail Stop EX-13
Olympia, WA 98504
(206)753-2448

Source for the list of rare, endangered, and threatened plants of Washington.

Wyoming

Wyoming Native Plant Society
P.O. Box 1417
Cheyenne, WY 82003

Publishes WNPS Newsletter. Sponsors annual field trip.

Wyoming Natural Diversity Database
3165 University Station
Laramie, WY 82071
(307)766-3441

National Organizations

American Horticultural Society
7931 East Boulevard Drive
Alexandria, VA 22308
(707)768-5700
1-800-777-7931

Publishes American Horticulturalist.

American Rock Garden Society
c/o Buffy Parker
15 Fairmead Road
Darien, CT 06820
(203)655-2750

Publishes The Bulletin of the American Rock Garden Society. *Twentynine chapters in North America.*

Canada Wildflower Society
75 Ternhill Crescent
North York, Ontario M3C 2E4

Publishes Wildflower. *Conducts a native plant seed exchange for members, supports wildflower conservation projects, has local chapters.*

Center for Plant Conservation
125 Arbor Way
Jamaica Plain, MA 02130
(617)524-6988

Conservation Foundation/
    World Wildlife Fund
1250 24th Street N.W.
Suite 500
Washington, DC 20037
(202)293-4800

Environmental Defense Fund
444 Park Avenue South
New York, NY 10016
(212)686-4191

National Wildflower Research Center
2600 FM 973 North
Austin, TX 78725
(512)929-3600

Publishes Wildflower. *Conducts research on native plants. Information clearing house. Phone hotline on Texas wildflowers in the spring.*

National Xeriscape Council, Inc.,
P.O. Box 163172
Austin, TX 78757

Publishes Xeriscape News. *State branches; 36 state educational programs.*

The Nature Conservancy
1815 North Lynn Street
Arlington, VA 22209
(703)841-5300

Operation Wildflower
National Council of State Garden
    Clubs
Mrs. Norman Collard, Chairman
Box 860
Pocasset, MA 02559

Publishes Columbine. *State and regional chapters. Works with Department of Transportation to plant wildflowers along highways.*

Soil and Water Conservation Society
7515 Northwest Ankeny Road
Ankeny, IA 50021

U.S. Fish and Wildlife Service
Office of Endangered Species
Washington, D.C. 20240

References

Art, H.W., 1986. *A Garden of Wild-flowers.* Garden Way Publishing/Storey Communications, Pownal, VT. 290 pp.

An illustrated guide to 101 native North American species and how to grow them.

Art, H.W., 1988. *Creating a Wildflower Meadow.* Garden Way Publishing/Storey Communications, Pownal, VT. 32 pp.

A Garden Way Publishing Bulletin on grasses and wildflowers suitable for North American meadows.

Art, H.W., 1990. *The Wildflower Gardener's Guide: California, Desert Southwest, and Northern Mexico Edition.* Garden Way Publishing/Storey Communications, Pownal, VT. 176 pp.

A guide on how to grow 34 species native to the Southwest. Illustrated with color photographs and superb line drawings.

Bailey, L.H., 1935. *The Standard Cyclopedia of Horticulture.* MacMillan, New York, NY. 3639 pp.

A classic gardening encyclopedia containing information on numerous native wildflowers as well as domesticated species.

Bakker, E., 1971. *An Island Called California.* U. California Press, Berkeley, CA. 361 pp.

A superb, readable introduction to the various types of vegetation in California.

California Native Plant Society, 1977. *Native Plants: A Viable Option.* California Native Plant Society, Sacramento, CA. 213 pp.

Suggestions for gardening with native plant species.

Clark, L.J., 1973. *Wildflowers of British Columbia.* Gray's Publishing, Ltd., Sidney, BC. 591 pp.

A large-format book with color photographs and detailed descriptions of northwestern wildflowers.

Clements, F.E. & E.S. Clements, 1928. *Rocky Mountain Flowers.* H.W. Wilson Co., New York, NY. 390 pp.

A classic guide for "plant-lovers and plant-users" that is out of print, but worth trying to find in the library or used book stores.

Collard, L.R., ed., 1985. *Wildflower Culture Guide.* National Council of State Garden Clubs, Inc., St. Louis, MO. 44 pp.

Articles on wildflower culture, wildflower gardens, and "Operation Wildflower."

Craighead, J.J., F.C. Craighead, Jr., & R.J. Davis, 1963. *A Field Guide to Rocky Mountain Wildflowers.* Houghton Mifflin, Boston, MA. 275 pp.

The Peterson Field Guide Series book for the region from northern Arizona and New Mexico to British Columbia.

Crittenden, M. & D. Telfer, 1975., *Wildflowers of the West.* Celestial Arts Press, Millbrae, CA. 199 pp.

A useful field guide to western wildflowers organized by flower characteristics.

Crockett, J.U. & O.E. Allen, 1977. *Wildflower Gardening.* Time-Life Books, Alexandria, VA. 160 pp.

Coast-to-coast examples of natives for the garden, with color illustrations.

Emery, D.E., 1988. *Seed Propagation of Native California Plants.* Santa Barbara Botanic Garden, Santa Barbara, CA. 118 pp.

An excellent book listing many native woody and herbaceous plants with recommended treatments for seed germination.

Foster, H.L., 1982. *Rock Gardening.* Timber Press, Portland, OR. 466 pp.

A reprint of the 1968 classic guide to growing alpine plants and other wildflowers in American gardens.

Fitzharris, 1986. *Wildflowers of Canada.* Oxford U. Press, Toronto, Ontario. 156 pp.

A handsome book with basic information about common wildflowers and superb color photographs.

Franklin, J.F. & C.T. Dyrness, 1973. *Natural Vegetation of Oregon and Washington.* Pacific Northwest Forest and

Range Experiment Station, Forest Service, U.S. Department of Agriculture [*General Technical Report PNW-8.*] 417 pp.

A technical, but readable, survey of the vegetation of the Pacific Northwest.

Gilby, H.M. & L.J. Dennis, 1967. *Handbook of Northwestern Plants.* Oregon State U. Bookstore, Corvallis, OR. 505 pp.

Descriptions of common plants, some illustrated with line drawings.

Hartmann, H.T. & D.E. Kester, 1975. *Plant Propagation, 3rd Edition.* Prentice-Hall, Englewood Cliffs, NJ. 662 pp.

A standard text about plant propagation.

Hill, L., 1985. *Secrets of Plant Propagation.* Garden Way Publishing, Pownal, VT. 168 pp.

How to propagate woody and herbaceous plants.

Hull, H.S., ed., 1982. *Handbook on Gardening with Wildflowers.* Brooklyn Botanic Garden, Brooklyn, NY. [B.B.G. *Plants & Gardens* 18(1).] 85 pp.

A variety of articles about native plant gardening.

Jacob, W. & I. Jacob, 1985. *Gardens of North America and Hawaii.* Timber Press, Portland, OR. 368 pp.

A useful cross-continent guide to gardens and arboreta with short descriptions and helpful state maps.

Johnson, L.B. & C.B. Less, 1988. *Wildflowers Across America.* National Wildflower Research Center & Abbeyville Press, New York, NY. 309 pp.

A coffee-table book with exciting and elegant color photographs of native and exotic wildflowers.

Klinka, K., V.J. Karajina, A Ceska, and A.M. Scagel, 1989. *Indicator Plants of Coastal British Columbia.* U. British Columbia Press, Vancouver, BC. 288 pp.

An information-filled guide to native plants of the Pacific Northwest, illustrated with color photographs.

Kruckeberg, A.R., 1982. *Gardening with Native Plants of the Pacific Northwest.* U. Washington Press, Seattle, WA. 252 pp.

Trees, shrubs, and perennial native plants, richly illustrated.

Martin, A.C., H.S. Zim, & A.L. Nelson, 1951. *American Wildlife and Plants.* Dover, New York, NY. 500 pp.

While not a book about wildflower gardening, this book is quite helpful in planning gardens to attract various wildlife species.

Martin, L.C., 1986. *The Wildflower Meadow Book.* East Woods Press, Charlotte, NC. 303 pp.

A coast-to-coast treatment of native and exotic wildflowers that grow in fields and meadows.

McGourty, F., 1978. *Ground Covers and Vines.* Brooklyn Botanic Garden, Brooklyn, NY. [B.B.G. *Plants & Gardens* 32(3).] 80 pp.

A useful booklet with articles on both native and exotic plants used as ground covers.

Moore, M., 1979. *Medicinal Plants of the Mountain West.* Museum of New Mexico Press, Santa Fe, NM. 200 pp.

An intriguing book detailing the medicinal properties of many wildflowers.

Munz, P.A., 1963. *California Mountain Wildflowers.* U. California Press, Berkeley, CA. 122 pp.

A guide to the common wildflowers of the Sierra Nevada and montane regions of California, some illustrated with color photographs.

National Wildflower Research Center, 1989. *Wildflower Handbook.* Texas Monthly Press, Austin, TX. 337 pp.

A very useful reference on wildflowers, where to purchase them, and where to obtain further information about them.

Niehaus, T.F. & C.L. Ripper, 1976, *A Field Guide to Pacific States Wildflowers.* Houghton Mifflin, Boston, MA. 432 pp.

The Peterson Field Guide Series edition for California to Washington and east to Utah.

Ornduff, R., 1974. *An Introduction to California Plant Life.* U. California Press, Berkeley, CA. 152 pp.

An excellent short guide to the diverse plant communities of California.

Parsons, M.E., 1966. *The Wildflowers of California.* Dover, New York, NY. 425 pp.

A reprint of the 1907 classic covering 666 different native California species, some with elegant illustrations.

Phillips, J., 1987. *Southwestern Landscaping with Native Plants.* Museum of New Mexico Press, Santa Fe, NM. 140 pp.

A helpful guide to planning and planting xeriscapes.

Porsild, A.E., 1979. *Rocky Mountain Wild Flowers.* National Museums of Canada & Parks Commission, Ottawa, Ontario. 454 pp.

A richly illustrated guide to wildflowers common to the Canadian Rockies. Color photographs.

Ray, M.H. & R.P. Nicholls, 1988. *The Traveller's Guide to American Gardens.* U. North Carolina Press, Chapel Hill, NC. 375 pp.

A state-by-state guide to gardens in the United States.

Ramaley, F., 1927. *Colorado Plant Life.* U. Colorado Press, Boulder, CO. 299 pp.

Out of print, but worth searching for this information-filled guide to many species of Rocky Mountain wildflowers.

Sawyers, C.E., ed, 1989. *Gardening with Wildflowers & Native Plants.* Brooklyn Botanic Garden, Brooklyn, NY. [B.B.G. *Plants & Gardens* 45(1).] 104 pp.

A variety of articles about native plant gardening.

Schmidt, M.G., 1980. *Growing California Native Plants.* U. California Press, Berkeley, CA. 366 pp.

A comprehensive treatment of California wildflowers and woody perennials. A classic.

Smith, G.S., 1989. *Mammoth Lakes Sierra: A Handbook for Roadside and Trail.* Genny Smith Books, Mammoth Lakes, CA. 224 pp.

A wonderful guide to the wildflowers, birds, geology, and more in the High Sierra.

Steffek, E.F., 1983. *The New Wild Flowers and How to Grow Them.* Timber Press, Portland, OR. 186 pp.

A sampling of wildflowers from North America, with useful tables of species from various regions and habitats.

Sullivan, G.A. & R.H. Dailey, 1981. *Resources on Wildflower Propagation.* National Council of State Garden Clubs, Inc., St. Louis, MO. 331 pp.

Contains a wealth of technical information about plants native to various regions of North America.

Sunset Books, 1988. *Sunset Western Garden Book.* Lane Publishing, Menlo Park, CA. 592 pp.

An excellent resource book for gardeners from the Rockies to the Pacific. Treats both native and exotic species with great care.

Weber, W.A., 1976. *Rocky Mountain Flora.* Colorado Associated U. Press, Boulder, CO. 479 pp.

A manual for the serious botanist, this book has helpful taxonomic keys and ample line drawings to identify many species.

Wilson, W.H.W., 1984. *Landscaping with Wildflowers and Native Plants.* Ortho Books, San Francisco, CA. 96 pp.

Listings of native plants for various regions and habitats.

Young, J.A. & C.G. Young, 1986. *Collecting, Processing, and Germinating Seeds of Wildland Plants.* Timber Press, Portland, OR. 236 pp.

Glossary

Annual. A plant whose life cycle from seed to mature plant, producing flowers, fruits and seeds, is completed in a single growing season. After seeds are produced, the plant usually dies.

Anther. A pollen-producing sac attached to the filament in the male portion of a flower.

Axil. The point of attachment between stem and leaf.

Basal rosette. An arrangement of leaves radiating from a short stem at the ground surface. Most biennials have a rosette form during their first growing season.

Biennial. A plant whose life cycle extends over two growing seasons. The first year the seed germinates, producing a seedling that usually remains short over the winter. The second growing season the seedling rapidly elongates, flowers, produces seeds, and then dies.

Bolting. The rapid elongation and flowering of biennials during their second growing season.

Boreal. Pertaining to regions of the northern hemisphere that have cold winters and forests dominated by coniferous species.

Bract. A modified leaflike structure, often resembling a petal, surrounding a flower or flower cluster.

Bulb. A fleshy rootstock composed of leaf bases or scaly leaves.

Bunch grasses. Species of grass that form distinct clumps or bunches as they grow, in contrast to the sod-forming grasses usually grown for lawns.

Calyx. The collective term for the sepals of a flower.

Capsule. A dry fruit that splits open to release its seeds.

Chaparral. Thickets of fire-adapted shrubs and small trees that develop in regions with hot dry summers and mild wet winters.

Charate. The charred remains of burned chaparral plants.

Coastal prairie. A natural grassland that develops near the Pacific Coast, usually on south-facing slopes that burn frequently.

Complete flowers. Flowers with sepals, petals, stamens, and a pistil all present.

Composite flower. A flower made up of many individual florets clustered into a common head, as is typical in members of the aster family.

Compound leaf. A leaf that is divided into two or more separate leaflets.

Corm. A fleshy rootstock formed by a short, thick, underground stem.

Corolla. The collective term for the petals of a flower.

Crest. A ridge of tissue.

Deciduous. Pertaining to plant parts, usually leaves, that are shed annually.

Desert. An ecosystem that develops in regions with annual precipitation of less than 10 inches, usually dominated by widely spaced shrubs and, where winters are mild, succulent species.

Disc flower (disc floret). One of the small, tubular flowers that form the central disc of flower heads in many members of the aster family.

Dissected. Deeply divided or split into lobes.

Dormancy. The resting or inactive phase of plants or seeds. Dormancy of shoots is usually in response to unfavorable environmental conditions. The breaking of seed dormancy requires moisture and sometimes cold tempertures and abrasion of the seed coat.

Elaiosome. An oily, starchy appendage on some seeds that attracts ants and other insects, which act as disperal agents.

Entire. A leaf margin that is smooth and lacking teeth.

Fibrous roots. A root system with many thin or branched root elements.

Filament. The anther-bearing stalk of a stamen.

Firescaping. A landscaping technique in which fire-resistant species are planted in close proximity to dwellings and other structures in fire-prone regions.

Floret. One of the small flowers that is clustered together forming the composite flower head in members of the aster family. Florets may be either tubular disc florets or straplike ray florets.

Flowering shoot. A stem that produces flowers.

Flower head. A cluster of florets or small flowers gathered together on a common receptacle, typically found in members of the aster family.

Forcing. Inducing a perennial to flower out of season. Forcing often involves artificial chilling followed by warming the plant.

Germination. The breaking of dormancy in seeds or the sprouting of pollen grains deposited on a stigma.

Habitat. The kind of environment inhabited by a particular species.

Half-hardy. An annual plant that is sown in early spring and flowers in summer.

Hardiness zone. An index relating geographic regions to a plant's ability to withstand minimum winter temperatures. Hardiness zones developed by the U.S. Department of Agriculture range from zone 1, with a minimum temperature of −50°F, to zone 10, with minimum temperatures of 30 to 40°F.

Hardy annual. An annual plant whose seeds can withstand subfreezing winter temperatures and whose seedlings can withstand spring frosts.

Hardy perennial. A perennial plant that is not permanently injured or killed by subfreezing temperatures.

Herbaceous. Plants that lack woody tissues and therefore "die back" to the soil surface at the end of the growing season.

Humus. Soft brown or black amorphous substance formed through the decomposition of leaves, wood, and other organic materials.

Innoculant. A commercially formulated strain of rhizobium added to the soil to aid in the establishment of various members of the bean family.

Inoculation. The addition of rhizobia to the soil.

Involucre. A whorl of leafy bracts surrounding composite flower heads such as those in the aster family.

Keel. The lower, pouchlike lip of flowers of certain members of the bean family. The keel is formed by the fusion of two petals.

Leaflets. The individual segments of a compound leaf.

Legume. A dry, flattened pod fruit that splits open at both edges when mature, as is found in members of the bean family. The term is also applied to the species of the bean family.

Long-day plant. A plant that flowers in response to the short nights of late spring and early summer.

Moist chilling treatment. A means of enhancing the germination of some seeds by storing them under moist conditions at low temperatures prior to planting them.

Montane. Pertaining to mountain environments, usually below the timberline.

Nodules. Outgrowths on the roots of plants in the bean family that are inhabited by nitrogen-fixing microorganisms known as rhizobia.

Non-flowering shoot. A stem that does not produce flowers; a vegetative shoot.

Ovary. The swollen base of a pistil, containing ovules. The ripening ovary, which is sometimes fused to the receptacle, becomes the fruit.

Ovules. The female sex cells that become seeds following fertilization.

Palmate. A pattern of compound leaflets or leaf venation, with elements radiating from a central point.

Peduncle. The main flowering stalk of a plant.

Perennial. A plant whose life cycle extends for an indefinite period beyond two growing seasons. These plants generally do not die following flowering.

Perfect flowers. Flowers with both stamens and a pistil, but lacking either sepals and/or petals.

Petal. A modified leaf attached to the receptacle outside the stamens and inside the calyx. Petals are usually showy and serve to attract pollinators to the flower.

Petiole. The stalk that attaches a leaf to a stem.

pH. A measure of the acidity/alkalinity of a substance ranging from 0 (strongly acidic) to 14 (strongly alkaline), with 7 being neutral.

Pistil. The female sexual part of a flower, consisting of the stigma, style, and ovary.

Plugs. A method of propagation by planting individual seeds in specially designed trays with small indentations. The root system of the seedlings fills the hole, forming a plug that can be easily removed and planted where desired.

Pollen. The powdery material produced in anthers, containing the male sex cells of flowering plants.

Pollination. The transfer of pollen from an anther to a stigma.

Propagation. Increasing the numbers of plants through seeds, cuttings, or divisions.

Pulvinus. A small, bulbous organ at the base of a petiole that controls the sun-tracking movement of leaves.

Ray flower (ray floret). One of the small flowers with a straplike petal, usually arranged in rings around the margin of flower heads in members of the aster family.

Receptacle. The fleshy tissue at the tip of a flower stalk to which flower parts are attached. Different species may have receptacles that are positioned below the ovary, form a cup around the ovary, or completely enclose the ovary.

Rhizobia. Microorganisms that inhabit nodules on the roots of members of the bean family. These organisms have the ability to take nitrogen from the air and create nitrogen compounds, usable by their host plants.

Rhizome. A horizontal, usually branched, underground stem with buds and roots.

Root division. Propagating plants by cutting vertically between root segments.

Root rot. Plant diseases, usually caused by fungi, that lead to the degeneration of roots.

Rootstock. An underground stem of a perennial plant with its associated buds and roots.

Runner. A thin, creeping, horizontal stem that trails along the surface of the ground and gives rise to small plants.

Scape. A leafless stem bearing a cluster of flowers.

Scarification. Abrasion of the seed coat allowing the passage of water and oxygen into the seed, thereby enhancing germination in some species.

Seed coat. The outer protective covering of a seed.

Sepal. A modified leaf that forms the covering of a flower bud. Sepals are attached to the outer margin of the receptacle and are usually green. However, in some species the sepals are brightly colored and resemble petals.

Shoot. The aboveground or stem portion of a plant that bears leaves, buds, and flowers.

Shoot bud. A bud that develops into stem and leaf tissue.

Short-day plant. A plant that flowers in response to the long nights of fall or early spring.

Simple flower. A solitary flower borne on a single stem.

Slip. An old-fashioned name for a cutting used for propagation.

Sods. A method of propagation by densely planting seeds in flats or trays. The root systems of the seedlings intertwine, allowing the sod to be removed in a single piece and planted where desired.

Softwood cutting. A propagation technique of cutting green, rapidly growing portions of stems while they are pliable.

Spadix. A fleshy, spindle-shaped column bearing flowers in members of the arum family.

Spathe. A large, leafy bract that frequently envelops the spadix in members of the arum and other plant families.

Stamen. The male sexual part of a flower consisting of an anther and a filament.

Stigma. The top surface of a pistil upon which pollen grains are deposited.

Stolon. A thin, underground runner.

Stratification. Chilling seeds to enhance their germination.

Style. The portion of the pistil connecting the stigma and the ovary.

Taproot. A thick, strongly vertical root, usually extending to considerable depth, for example, the carrot.

Tender annual. An annual plant whose seedlings are killed by spring frosts.

Tender perennial. Perennial plants that are permanently damaged or killed by subfreezing temperatures.

True root. The descending, underground portion of a plant that is specialized to provide support and absorb water and nutrients. True roots usually lack buds.

Tuber. A rootstock formed by a fleshy, swollen tip of a stolon.

Tule meadow. Wetland vegetation interspersed in valley grasslands and dominated by tule (bulrush) and cattails.

Vernal pools. "Hog wallows" or depressions that collect water over the winter rainy season and form temporary pools. As pools dry out over the spring various wildflowers bloom at their edges.

Vernalization. The cold treatment needed by some fall-germinating plants to promote flowering the following spring.

Weed. Any plant that grows where it is not wanted.

Wetlands. An area of low-lying land with soils that are submerged or wet for a significant portion of each year.

Wildflower. An herbaceous plant capable of growing, reproducing, and becoming established without cultivation.

Winter annual. An annual plant that usually germinates in the fall, overwinters as a seedling, and flowers the following spring.

Woody. Having hard, tough tissues that persist from year to year and are capable of producing shoot or flower buds. Woody plants also have the capacity to increase in diameter from year to year.

Xeriscaping. A landscaping technique in which water consumption is reduced by planting drought-resistant species, matching water requirements of landscape plants to available soil moisture, using high-efficiency irrigation systems, and other water-conserving techniques.

Index

Boldface numbers, such as **127**, indicate that illustrations or tables appear on that page.

Forests
  evergreen, 3-4
  fires, 3-4
  north coastal, 3-4
  species, 82-101
  subalpine, 4
  western montane, species, 102-125
Frost-free period, 39, **61**. *See also* Hardiness zones
Fruit, 30, 33
Fumigants, 27

G

Gaillarde. See Blanketflower
Gaillardia aristata. See Blanketflower
Gaillardia. *See* Blanketflower
Gambel's oak, 141
Gardens
  alpine, **127**
  botanical, 16-17
  butterfly, 18-20, **19**, **20**
  container, 21-22
  foothill, **141**
  horticultural, 18-22
  hummingbird, 18-20, **19**
  landscapes, 22-28
  montane, **103**
  natural, 22-28
  Pacific slope and coast, **83**
  requiring little water, 22-23
  rock, 21, 24
  seaside, 23-24
  theme, 18-28
  See also Meadows
Gaultheria shallon. See Salal
Genetic factors, and flowering season, 37-38
Geum triflorum. See Prairie smoke
Giant evening primrose, 24, **67**, **83**, 92, **93**
Giant sequoias, 4
Giant trillium, 14, 24, **69**, **83**, 100, **101**
Gilia aggregata. See Scarlet gilia
Glacier lily. *See* Yellow fawn lily
Godetia amoena. See Farewell-to-spring
Godetia. *See* Farewell-to-spring
Golden currant, 103

Grasses
  alpine, 4
  bunchgrasses, 5, 6
  native western, 25
  for a wildflower meadow, 25-26
  See also Meadows
Grasslands, 6
Great willow herb. *See* Fireweed
Ground covers, 20-21, 22. *See also* Meadows
Gumbo evening primrose. *See* Tufted evening primrose

H

Hardiness zones, 39-41, **42**, **62**
Harebell, 21, **24**, **26**, **74**, **127**, 128, **129**
Heath shrubs, 5
Height, 30, **32**
Herald-of-summer. *See* Farewell-to-spring
Herbicides, 27, 49-50
Hierba de Santiago. See Giant evening primrose
Highways, beautifying, 17
Hooker's evening primrose. *See* Giant evening primrose
Horticultural gardens, 18-22
Horticultural organizations, 17
Horticultural Society of London, 7
Household pets, 50
Hummingbirds, 8-9
  garden for, 18-20
Hymenoxys grandiflora. See Old-man-of-the-mountain

I

Immortelle. See Pearly everlasting
Indian blanket. *See* Blanketflower
Indian paintbrushes, 11
Indian ricegrass, 25, **26**
Insects, 50
Ipomopsis aggregata. See Scarlet gilia
Iris douglasiana. See Douglas's iris

J

June grass, 25, **26**

Juniper, 5, 141
Juniperus monosperma. See Juniper
Juniperus occidentalis. See Juniper
Juniperus osteosperma. See Juniper

K

Kalmia microphylla. See Alpine laurel
Kings crown, 126
Kinnikinnik, 102
Koeleria cristata. See June grass
Krummholz, 4

L

Lamb's tongue. *See* Yellow fawn lily
Lance-leaved coreopsis, 140
Landscapes, 22-28
Large-leaved lupine. *See* Washington lupine
Laws, wildflower protection, 12, 13
Legumes, 54-55
Leopard lily, 21, **66**, **83**, 88, **89**
Lepachys columnaris. See Mexican hat
Lewis, Meriwether, 6-7
Lewis & Clark expedition, wildflowers discovered by, 6-7
Lewisia rediviva. See Bitterroot
Life everlasting. *See* Pearly everlasting
Light conditions, 39, **40**
Lilium pardalinum. See Leopard lily
Lin de Lewis. See Blue flax
Linnea borealis. See Twinflower
Linum lewisii. See Blue flax
Linum perenne ssp. lewisii. See Blue flax
Lithocarpus densiflorus. See Tan oak
Little bluestem, 25
Little pink elephants. *See* Elephant-heads
Lobelia cardinalis. See Cardinal flower
Local conditions, and flowering season, 37
Lodgepole pine, 4
Lobelia cardinalis. See Cardinal flower
"Long-day" plants, 37
Lupinus polyphyllus. See Washington lupine
Luzula spicata. See Rushes

Propagation, 51-58. *See also* specific
    methods of propagation
Pseudotsuga menziesii. See Douglas fir

Q

Queens crown, 126
Quercus gambelii. See Gambel's oak

R

Rain. *See* Precipitation
Ratibida columnaris. See Mexican hat
Ratibida columnifera. See Mexican hat
Ray flowers, **29**, 30
Receptacle, **29**
Red fir, **4**
Red Mexican hat. *See* Mexican hat
Redwood sorrel, 7, 21, **22**, **67**, **83**, 94,
    95
Rhizobia inoculants, 54-55
Rhizomes, **34**
    division, 55, **56**
Rhodiola integrifolia. See Kings crown
Rhododendron, 82-83
Rhododendron macrophyllum. See
    Rhododendron
Ribes aureum. See Golden currant
Rock clematis, 103
Rock gardens, 21, 24
Rocky Mountain beeplant, 7, **77**, 142,
    143. *See also* Cleome
Rocky Mountain columbine. *See*
    Colorado columbine
Rocky Mountain maple, 141
Rocky Mountain penstemon, **24**, **74**,
    103, 124, **125**, 140
Rootstock division, 55-57, **56**
Root systems, 33, **34**
Rosebay. *See* Fireweed
Rubrus parviflorus. See Thimbleberry
Rudbeckia hirta. See Black-eyed Susan
Runners, 33, **34**
    division, 55, **56**
Rushes, **4**
Russell, George, 7
Russell hybrid lupines, 7
Rydbergia grandiflora. See Old-man-of-
    the-mountain

Rydbergia. See Old-man-of-the-
    mountain

S

Sagebrush, 141
Salal, 83
Scarification, 52-53
Scarlet gilia, 7, 8, **19**, 21, **78**, **141**,
    146, **147**
Scotch bellflower. *See* Harebell
Seaside gardens, 23-24
Sedum lanceolatum. See Yellow stone-
    crop
Seeds, 33, 51-52
    collecting from the wild, 14
    commercial mixes, 15
    formation of, 30, 33
    heat treatments, 53
    light or dark treatments, 53
    planting techniques, 53-55
    scarification, 52-53
    storing, 51-52
    stratification, 52
    suppliers, 14-15, 16
Sepals, **29**, 30
Sequoia-dendron giganteum. See Giant
    sequoias
Sequoia sempervirens. See Coast red-
    woods
Sheep fescue, 25
"Short-day" plants, 38
Shrubs, 5, 6
    for alpine regions, 127
    for foothill regions, 140-141
    north coastal, 82-83
    for western montane forest, 103
    for xeriscaping, 23
Sidalcea malvaeflora. See Checker
    bloom
Sideoats grama, 25
Silene acaulis. See Moss campion
Silver-leaf. *See* Pearly everlasting
Simple flowers, **29**, 30
Sitka spruce, 3
Skunk flower. *See* Scarlet gilia
Skunk polemonium. *See* Sky pilot
Sky pilot, 9, **24**, **77**, **127**, 138, **139**

Skyrocket gilia. *See* Scarlet gilia
Slope, and flowering season, 37
Slugs, 50
Small grape. *See* Oregon grape
Smilacina racemosa. See Western
    Solomon's seal
Smilacine à grappes. See Western
    Solomon's seal
Snails, 50
Snow lily. *See* Yellow fawn lily
Snowplant, 11
Sods, 54
Soil
    and flowering season, 37
    mixes, 53-54
    moisture conditions, 39-43, **44**, 82
    pH, 43-47, **46**
        changing, 48-49
        measuring, 47-48
    potting, 53-54
Sphaeralcea coccinea. See Desert
    mallow
Spreading phlox, 126-127
Stamen, **29**, 30
Stem cuttings, **57**-58
Stemless evening primrose. *See* Tufted
    evening primrose
Stigma, **29**, 30
Stipa spartea. See Porcupinegrass
Stolons, 33, **34**
    division, 55, **56**
Stratification, 52
Style, **29**, 30
Subalpine fir, 4
Subalpine forests, 4
Sulfur flower. *See* Sulfur-flowered
    eriogonum
Sulfur-flowered buckwheat. *See*
    Sulfur-flowered eriogonum
Sulfur-flowered eriogonum, **19**, 21, **75**,
    127, 132, **132**, 140
Summer's darling. *See* Farewell-to-
    spring
Sun god. *See* Old-man-of-the-
    mountain
Suppliers, 14-15, 16
Sword fern, 82